THE SANITY INSPECTOR

When Sir Henry Souvenir (1526–1587) at last returned to the court of Queen Elizabeth from his ten-year tour of the Orient, he little thought that their opening exchange would pass into history.

"What have you brought for me?" asked his queen.

"It's a box made from the liver of an elephant, your majesty," replied Sir Henry, "wrought in strange fashion by the natives and covered in sea-shells. You can keep fags in it."

"Where did you get it?" she inquired.

"I can't remember," he said.

The Sanity Inspector

Alan Coren

CORONET BOOKS
Hodder and Stoughton

First published in 1974 in Great Britain by
Robson Books Limited

Coronet edition 1976
Second impression 1976
Third impression 1976
Fourth impression 1976

The author would like to thank the proprietors
of *Punch* magazine for permission to reproduce
material in this book.

Printed and bound in Great Britain for
Coronet Books, Hodder and Stoughton,
London
by Richard Clay (The Chaucer Press), Ltd.,
Bungay, Suffolk

ISBN 0 340 19912 1

For Giles

Marketing

Contents

Foreword

We had an au pair once, called Ilse. She claimed to have been a biochemist, originally, but the magic went out of it. Anyway, that was the gist: my German was shaky, and it shook in time to her English. So Ilse came to us, and she used to eat chops in the small hours and sleep in a hat. Once, she arrived home at seven a.m. carrying a gate. Who am I to say there was anything wrong with her? I know little of the effects on the psyche when biochemistry goes sour.

She phoned me one day at the office. We were putting in a new bathroom at home, and officials with clipboards kept coming to look at it. Ilse liked to check them out with me, in case the clipboards were a mask for rape. So I picked up the phone on this occasion, and Ilse said: "Is coming the Sanity Inspector". I told her that was fine, and make sure he shuts the door after him. After I put the phone down, I thought about it for a while.

Maybe he really was.

But she was still there in the evening, so he hadn't come for her. Either that, or she had passed the test. It isn't the sort of thing you ask anyone, so I never mentioned it again. Besides, there was always the chance that he had in fact come for me; and, finding me out, had gone away to bide his time. Maybe I'll meet him in Samarra.

If I do, I'll give him this book, in the hope it will help him to understand that it wasn't just me. It was the times I lived in. And that he and I were in the same business, really.

AC

Forelock And After

I sometimes feel my life is being organised by the Foreign Office. They never tell me about it, of course; it is merely that in some dusty Whitehall priest's hole beneath the wormy stairs, an elderly minor official sits between a brace of dented wire trays into one of which comes information on my life and out of the other of which go his copper-plate recommendations as to what should be done with me.

I identify the FO as the secret arbiter of my destiny only because of what I already know of its operations, and how well its methods fit with the weird movement of my life. A number of my contemporaries actually chose to go into the Foreign Office: if they read Arabic at university, they were swooped on by Whitehall and sent to Japan; if they read Japanese, they were sent on a special FO training course to learn German, and subsequently placed in Kampala; if their predilection and brilliance were commercial, they were given posts where political expertise was the sole requirement; if they were geographers, they were despatched to found hospitals or advise on fowl pest. In short, as soon as they had completed the long and arduous process of learning something, it was no longer required. They were in a state of permanent dynamic obsolescence.

My entire life has been like that.

When I was young, and had hair, the fashion was to cut it as close to the skull as possible; when I grew older, the fashion was to wear it long and flowing, by which time most of it had fallen out. When I was likewise young, and thin, all clothes were made for fleshy middle-aged men; and I would walk the streets in something double-breasted and full of breeze, looking like an unguyed wigwam. Now I am older and fleshier, all the clothes are made for malnourished Watutsis, and I may be seen any day struggling up Fleet Street in my worsted bonds like a cocktail sausage with a hernia, in a hail of lethal buttons that would do credit to a New Orleans cop. When I was nineteen, and ravenous for debauchery, the prerequisites for a successful seducer were thirty-five years, at least, a wardrobe of light-weight suits, a deft hand with a martini, and a face upon which experience had etched its thrilling diary; as soon as I reached man's estate (at the exact moment, I understand, when I was standing in my tailor's and flipping through a swatch of rakish mohairs), the norm became a teenager in tattered denims over a Donald Duck vest who shaved with a tweezer and whose entrée to London's most desirable nubilia hung upon his ability to roll a joint with his left hand while unhooking a bra with his right.

Everything I ever learned, in fact, became outdated at the moment I finished learning it, and everything towards which I ever strove changed its terms in the very second at which I panted over the last ridge to stick my flag on it.

And in no area was this more true or more exasperating than in the loony maze of class. Because for a large and irretrievable chunk of my youth, when the rest of the neighbourhood was practising going in off the red or stretching the growing stomach for the lifetime of pints to come, I was studying how to become a gentleman; and when I got there (or as near as dammit, as we self-taught gentlemen may sometimes be heard to say), gentlemen were a joke. What I had always regarded as the class ladder turned out to be nothing but a treadmill. Worse, had I never changed, I'd be at the top now.

Take accent. In my early untrained years as a natural oik, given to finking deep foughts abaht making sunnink of meself and only using an aitch when I used the word haitch, the social exemplars at whom I set my cap (it had, of course, a peak stained and misshapen with years of tugging) spoke, as they haw-hawed around Princess Margaret or threw bread-rolls at Tommy Kinsman's drummer, in accents stropped to a deadly edge upon the belts of earls. It was an enunciation forged (in every sense) at Eton, buffed by the Guards (or, equally, guarded by the Buffs), and kept bright and sharp by a life of constant use. The accent was the first indication one had that one was in the presence of a gentleman; indeed, it was the first indication one had that one was *about* to be in the presence of a gentleman, since it invariably preceded him around corners, pitch being as important as pronunciation. More than a mere accent, it was actually the language of a race, the national characteristics of which were power, privilege, wealth, exclusivity, and a knack with the better class of dog. It was the accent with which politicians declared war and the public media delivered the plebs' pabulum, it was the voice of business and Empire and higher education, it was what one needed To Get On.

So I listened assiduously to Alvar Lidell and Joan Gilbert, and by this Linguaphonic method, I got fairly close to a passable imitation of it.

And as soon as I had got my glottis to handle the trickier syllables and semitones and at the moment when I was poised to round off the course by mastering my first public Haw, Haw, Haw, the entire edifice collapsed; Michael Wilding and Michael Denison were replaced by Michael Caine and Albert Finney, and there was scant place in smart society for the echoing Joyce Grenfell into which I had transformed myself. It had become not merely acceptable, but highly desirable, to be working-class, with all the colour and cachet with which the arts had invested it, so I had to go through my entire repertoire again knocking off the aitches, and it never came out right. There's nothing worse than being a parody of your real self because you've forgotten what your real self was. It all happened during my first year at Oxford, to which I'd gone trepidantly, trusting I could pass myself off as the necessary gentleman, and where all I ran into were gentlemen apologising for being same and trusting they could pass themselves off as the New Order.

It was at about this time that Holland Park Comprehensive opened its doors, offering men who felt uneasy about having gone to an old public school the opportunity of sending their children to a new public school. I, who had been to a state school hung with the secondhand trappings of a private school where kids from working-class homes had grafted onto them the paraphernalia and mores of Harry Wharton & Co, had missed the boat again. Just.

Likewise the groundplan for gentility of Mitford and Ross. Hardly had I programmed myself spontaneously to ask for lavatory and napkin, when England jumped an entire class division: not only were both lavatory and toilet eschewed in favour of a welter of synonyms like khazi, bog, loo, head, can, and so forth, but the napkin-serviette disappeared entirely at those fashionable spots where one might be lucky enough to rub up against a Bermondsey tellyman or Liverpudlian guitarist who wiped his mouth on his hat. Furthermore, on the night-scene, I who had painstakingly learned to foxtrot in full evening dress without removing my head on the knife-edge collar during a quick reverse telemark, discovered that all this, too, was now in vain, since what was de rigueur in those discotheques where one might get the chance to frug with a countess was overalls and a donkey-jacket with Wimpey embroidered on the back.

It was, of course, simply that the money was changing hands, and as impoverished nobs served cream teas in the crumbling west wings to chara-queues, men who had started with one gravel pit were to be found in Sotheby's engaged upon furnishing the yacht. Charmed circles buckled askew, and men were yanked off boards by their old school ties to make way for lads with chunky cufflinks who had perfected the reverse takeover at an age when their toney predecessor was worrying about holding his place in the First XV. So power and privilege shifted as the lease upon their foundations was transferred, and new positions with new heroes in them were established, and it came to matter not a whit that the Conservative Party was led by a man who will never be able to get How Now Brown Cow right, though he stand before his mirror from now till Doomsday.

And glad I am of it, really. I just wish they'd told me a little earlier about the way it was all going to turn out. I could have used that time and effort to better ends.

Still, that's yer bleeding Life all over, innit?

Let Us Now Phone Famous Men

A child's game, at root, like all good things. After all, could anything match that first fine discovery of the telephone and all it stood for? That first realisation that, contained within ten simple digits, lay the infinitely possible? Out there—the information seeped into the infant brain in all its diabolical clarity —lay six billion ears, all the people in the world, available for contact and mystery and insult, unable to resist the beckoning of one small and villainous forefinger. We used, my tiny evil friends and I, to congregate at the nearest parentless house, and dial into the void, and innocent mouths would answer, and gullible ears would wait. Ah, to be only eight and wield such limitless power over adults! To fell a vicar with a practised oath, to turn bass breathing on a solitary spinster, to order fourteen tons of coal from Rickett Cockerell and have it delivered to the schoolmaster of one's choice—what could match this for delirious joy? Only the pièce de résistance of scouring the phone-book for a citizen called Dumm or Barmie and phoning him to enquire if he was. What nights we spent in illicit spinnings of the dial, tottering helplessly about our living-rooms, gasping at our own wit and ingenuity and smashing our milk-teeth on the fender in the thrashing throes brought on by such hilarity!

I wonder, sometimes, if the men who were boys when I was a boy still do it. It's not a question you can ask of bald, august solicitors, of doctors nursing kids and mortgages, of paunched executives: but do they, a quarter of a century on, creep down. perhaps, at 4 a.m. and ring their enemies to offer six free foxtrot lessons, or scream indecencies at subscribers doomed to names like Bott and Hoare?

I thought of them last week, those tiny swine who helped mis-spend my youth. Because it suddenly occurred to me to crank the whole game up to a more sophisticated notch: perhaps it was the opening of direct dialling to New York, perhaps it was the acreage of puerile posters by which the Post Office whips us on to take advantage of their miracle offers, but, whatever the spur, I decided to spend the day trying to telephone the leaders of the world. Why not? After all, they had ears like anyone else, they had desks with phones on, they were put in power, more or less, by insignificant souls like me: surely they could set aside a few seconds for a chat, an exchange of gossip, an acknowledge-ment that the silent majority had a right, occasionally, to speak?

So I phoned Mao Tse-Tung.

"Who?" said the girl on 108 (International Directory En-quiries).

"He's the Chairman of the Chinese People's Republic," I said. "It's probably a Peking number."

There was a long silence. I could see her there, repolishing an immaculate nail, shoving a wayward curl back beneath her head-set, sucking a Polo, wondering whether she should go on the pill.

"I'll get the Supervisor," she said, finally.

"Nobody ever phones China," said the Supervisor.

"Why not?"

"I don't know," she said. Her voice was diamantine. "I only know why people phone places, I don't know why they don't, do I?"

Ruined by syntax, I pled help.

"You could phone the Chinese Chargé d'Affaires in London," she said. "The number is 580 7509."

580 7509 yielded a high-pitched moan. My Chinese may be less than flawless, but even I could tell that no human larynx was involved.

I phoned the Operator.

Who phoned the Engineer.

Whose Supervisor phoned me.

"It's NU," he said. For a moment, I felt excitingly privy to some piece of inside dope about Post Office/Chinese Legation affairs: clearly, from the man's weary voice, it was old Enn-Yu up to his tricks again, Enn-Yu the phone-bugger (I don't mean that the way it looks), the tamperer, the Red Guard saboteur; Enn-Yu, the man who had plagued the GPO for years with his intercepted calls and weird Oriental devices fitted out in the Legation basement.

"Who's Enn-Yu?" I said.

"Not In Use," he said, and a small world crashed. "They're always switching their lines down there. Every six weeks, they want a new phone number. Hang on," he said, and voices muttered in the background, and far bells rang. He came back. "It's 636 9756 this week," he said.

"Harro!" shouted a voice at 636 9756.

"Hallo," I said. "I want to know how I can telephone China."

"Why?"

"I want to speak to Chairman Mao."

"Why?"

"I have a personal message to deliver."

Breathing. Whispering. A new, more senior voice.

"Not possible terrephone China!" it shrieked. "Not possible terrephone Chairman! What you want?"

I explained again. It turned out that there were no lines between England and China. Nobody ever telephoned China. Nobody *would* ever telephone China.

"How do *you* speak to China?" I asked.

A third voice came on.

"GET OFF RINE!" it screamed. "GET OFF RINE QUICK NOW!"

And rang off. The whole thing had taken forty-seven minutes. More than enough time for thermonuclear gee-gaws to have wiped both Asia and Europe off the map. I knew the PM didn't have a hot line to Mao, and it bothered me.

I dialled again.

"Yes?" said 108.

"I'd like," I said, "to speak to Mr. Kosygin."

She muffled the phone inadequately.

"I think it's him again," I heard, distant and woolly. There was giggling. I waited. The Supervisor came on.

"Are you," she said, and the syllables fell like needles, "the gentleman who just wanted to speak to Mao Tse-Tung?"

"Yes," I said.

I sympathised. She had, I knew, a vision of this solitary loonie who had let himself loose on the telephonic world, prior, no doubt, to rape or suicide. I wondered if they were playing for time with their long, reflective pauses, trying to trace the call, trying to dispatch a van-load of GPO male nurses to my gate. But all she said was:

"Russian Inquiries are on 104."

"Have you got his address and phone number?" said 104.

"No," I said, "I thought you'd have it."

"They never send us directories," she said. "It's only them and the Rumanians that don't. Everyone else sends us their directories."

"Then how do you phone Russians?"

"You have to have their number. We keep," she grew confidential, "a list of hotels and factories, a few things like that. We're not supposed to, but we do. I've got the Kremlin number. Do you think that would do?"

"Yes, that sounds very good."

"There's an hour's delay to Moscow. I'll get them to ring you back, and he might come to the phone. That'd be nice, wouldn't it?"

"That would be very nice," I said. "In the meantime, as you're European Directory, could you get the Pope for me?"

"Oooh, you are *awful*!" she shrieked. Her voice faded, and I could just catch it explaining the situation to the other girls. Time passed. She came back.

"You're not going to say nothing dirty to them, are you?" she said. "Excuse me for asking, but we have to."

I reassured her.

"I'll have to keep your number by me," she said, "in case there's complaints, you know, afterwards, like. No offence

18

meant, but you'd be surprised how many people ring up foreigners and swear at them."

I agreed, wondering who. Insights were bursting in on every hand. It clearly wasn't all beer and skittles, being a world leader, trying to keep up the balance of payments and build new schools and hold back the opposition, with Englishmen phoning you up all hours of the day and night, shouting "Eff off!"

She gave me the Pope's residential number. I dialled direct, 01039 6 6982. It was engaged. Odd. Was he, perhaps, on The Other Line? Or just on the balcony, waving? I tried again, trembling slightly at his proximity—five hundred million subjects under his thumb, and that thumb about to curl over the receiver in response to a far, agnostic call.

"Allo."

"Your Holiness?"

Pause.

"Wod?"

"Am I speaking to the Pope? *Il Papa?*"

Scuffling.

"Allo, allo. Can I 'elp you?"

"May I speak to the Pope?"

A long, soft sigh, one of those very Italian sighs that express so much, that say *Ah, signor, if only this world were an ideal world, what would I not give to be able to do as you ask, we should sit together in the Tuscan sunshine, you and I, just two men together, and we should drink a bottle of the good red wine, and we should sing, ah, how we should sing, but God in His infinite wisdom has, alas, not seen fit to . .*

"Can the Pope," I said, determined, "come to the phone?"

"The Bobe never gum to the delephone, signor. Nod for you, nod for me, nod for Italians, nod for nobody. Is not bozzible, many regrets, 'Is 'Oliness never spig on delephone. You give me your name, I give mezzage to 'Is 'Oliness, 'e give you blezzing, okay?"

"Okay," I said. A blessing, albeit proxied, was something.

"Don menshnit," he said, kindly, and clicked off.

By great good fortune (or even the grace of God: who knows how quickly a Pope's blessing might work?), there was a different operator on 108 when I tried to reach Richard Nixon. He put me on to 107, who got me the White House in three minutes flat, which gave tricky Dicky a thick edge over Mao, Kosygin and Il Papa when it came to accessibility. I thought you'd like to know that, Dick, since I didn't get the chance to tell you myself. Accessibility, as Harry Truman might have said, stops here. Or almost here. The lady secretary at the White House was extremely kind, incredibly helpful and understanding; doubtless because, given America's readiness to empty magazines at those in power, you can't be too careful with nuts who phone up to speak to the President. Fob them off with a "Get lost!" one minute, and the next they're crouched on a nearby roof and pumping away with a mail-order Winchester. The President, she said, was down in Florida, at Key Biscayne, where his number was 305 358 2380; someone there would speak to me. They did, and they were just as syrupy and sympathetic, and who knows but that I mightn't have got into the Great Ear if I hadn't played one card utterly wrong? What happened was, the call from the Kremlin, booked, you'll remember, an hour before, suddenly came through on my other phone, and I was mug enough, drunk with bogus eminence, to say to the American voice:

"Sorry, can you hold on a sec, I've got Kosygin on the other line?"

It was a nice moment, of course, but that's as long as it lasted. America hung up. Tread carefully when you step among the great, friends, their corns are sensitive.

I rather liked the Kremlin.

"Is that Mister Coren?" they said.

It's no small thrill to think one's name has echoed down the corridors of Soviet power, from room to room, while nervous men, fearful of the punishment that follows bureaucratic cock-ups, have tried to find out who one is, and what one wants with the Prime Minister. After all, so much is secret, so much unknown. I might have been anybody, even the sort of Anybody whose whisper in a top ear could send whole switchboardsful of comrades to the stake. Who was this Coren, this cool, curt international voice who seemed to be on such good terms with Alexi N. Kosygin that he thought nothing of phoning him person-to-person? For men who remembered Lavrenti Beria, no kindness to strangers was too much. Which is no doubt why I actually got to Kosygin's private secretary, who was himself extremely civil.

"I merely want to present the Prime Minister with my good wishes," I told him.

He was heartbroken that the Prime Minister was inextricably involved at present, but swore to me that my message would be passed on immediately. And I have not the slightest doubt that it was. It's a long way to Siberia, after all, and the cattle-trains leave every hour, on the hour.

Which left me with just two numbers in my little black book: Havana 305 031 and Cairo 768944. It took me a day to get through to one, and three days to reach the other (all calls to Egypt are subject to censorship), and when I finally did make contact, Fidel and Anwar were, needless to say, busy elsewhere. Both, however, promised faithfully to ring me back, which is why I leave them till last. Courtesy I like. Not, though, that they actually *have* rung back, but who knows? Even now, the dark, dependable forefingers may be poised over their respective dials, groping along the cables for a chance to chew the fat and swop a joke or two. If not, and if they read this first, don't worry about it, lads. It's nothing urgent.

I just wanted to say hello.

What Every Schoolboy Knows

With the introduction of sex education into the curriculum of the under-tens, something is likely to happen to the whole fabric of the British school system. In fact, anything is.

The honeyed sun streamed through the double-glazed mock-mullions of St. Swine's Comprehensive, dappling the upturned faces of the two thousand pupils at morning assembly and making their little bloodshot eyes cringe back into their sallow bags. Many a tiny tongue was furred with the strain of a long night's practical homework, many a small hand trembled involuntarily, many a lustless head lolled on an aching shoulder, all passion spent.

As the last discordant notes of *How Sweet The Name Of Kinsey Sounds* died wearily away, the Headmaster rose, drew his dirty fawn raincoat more majestically around him, and, pausing only to fondle the Senior Mistress, cleared his scrawny throat.

"School," he began, in that distinguished whine so familiar to the smaller girls, on whom it was his habit to press boiled sweets, "I have one extremely pleasant duty to perform before we dismiss. As you know, this is the moment in Assembly at which we offer our thanks and congratulations to those whose achievements above and beyond the call of mere duty have brought honour to the fine name of St. Swine's. Today, I ask you to acknowledge in the traditional manner the success of J. Griswold of the Lower Sixth, through whose selfless and un-stinting efforts Millicent Foskett and Anona Rutt of Form 5a have both become pregnant."

The staff applauded vigorously, drumming excited feet upon

the echoing dais. The school, however, responded merely with a dutiful and brief clapping of limp hands.

Nobody liked a swot.

It was the shrieking laughter from the gymnasium changing-room that proved the illicit mob's undoing. As it rang across the playground and down the musky corridors of the school, it fell inevitably upon the tensed ear of the Senior PT Master, who sprang athletically from the Matron, grabbed his track-suit on the half-leap, and began sprinting towards the fearful noise of joy. He took the gym steps four at a time, as befitted a man who had outdistanced every husband in the neighbourhood, tore open the changing-room door, plunged through the mass of terror-stricken boys and dragged three soaking offenders with their hands upon the very taps out from the shining tiles.

They trembled before his fury, their sin pooling around their feet.

"You disgusting little pigs!" shrieked the Senior PT Master, shaking with such rage that the Matron's ear-ring disentangled itself from his sideburn and rolled away beneath a bench. "So this is what happens when my back is turned! An orgy! An—an unspeakable vileness! To think that St. Swine's boys should be found taking cold showers!"

Biggs of 3b, tiniest of the offenders, began to sob.

"It's—it's not my—f-f-fault, sir," he wept. "I c-c-couldn't help it!"

Veins twanged and knotted on the Master's temple.

"Couldn't help it, Biggs? *Couldn't help it?*" He bent his terrible face to the fast-blueing lecher. "How many times have you been told what a cold shower will do to a healthy young lad, Biggs? What will happen to you if you don't stop doing it?"

"I—I'll g-g-go b-blind, sir," sobbed Biggs.

"Right! And what else?"

"I'll b-b-break out in w-warts."

"And?"

"G-g-go bald. D-d-die in a loony bin."

The Senior PT Master straightened.

"This is the last time I'll tell you," he roared, and his little black eyes drilled into their very souls. "Don't think I don't understand a boy's problems. Don't think I don't know what it's like when the awful wicked urge to have a cold shower comes over a young man. But when that nasty desire takes its terrible hold on you, there's one thing you can do, isn't there? And that's go straight out and . . . what?"

"Get laid, sir!" screamed the boys.

"Right!" roared the Senior PT Master.

Biggs of 3b got home at four in the morning. His eyes rolled in their sockets like a couple of maraschino cherries, and a lard-like sheen coated his saffron skin. He was carrying an enormous teddy-bear, a deflated balloon, and a box of cheap cigars. He fell through the door, and fetched up, gasping, against a radiator. His parents were still up, waiting.

"Where you been this time?" asked his father.

"Educational outing," whispered Biggs of 3b, and dozed off.

"Where to?" shrieked his mother, shaking him.

Biggs of 3b woke.

"Take 'em off!" he yelled. "Take 'em off!"

"Where *to*, Nigel?"

The child licked his lips, regained a sort of consciousness.

"Been on a ramble," he muttered, "to the Greek Street Nudorium and Strip-o-rama. After that, we visited a Fräulein Sadie Bamboo. At least, 3b did. 3a had to try picking birds up on Clapham Common. They got a Proficiency Certificate exam next term. Norman Loom's gone off to Brighton with a retired Chief Petty Officer." The boy yawned. "Norman's working for a Special Paper."

"They're working the lad too hard," said his father to Mrs. Biggs. "All this learning. It don't make up for experience. Filling his brains up with stuff. I left school at fourteen and had Maureen Hodges in the bus-shelter. Getting out in the world, that's what does it."

"Werl, you weren't exactly an intellectual, were you?" said his wife. "More practical. Good with your hands."

"Good with my hands," nodded Mr. Biggs. "More practical. Now, Nigel," he said kindly to the boy, "off to bed."

Biggs of 3b shook his head wretchedly.

"Can't," he moaned. "Got to do my prep, haven't I? Got to stand up in class tomorrow and Describe In My Own Words Without Aid Of Diagrams, haven't I?"

"Oh," said his father.

"Oh," said his mother.

They looked bleakly at one another. His father sniffed.

"We've not got to help him with his homework again, have we?" he muttered.

His wife sighed heavily.

"We shouldn't stand in the way of his education," she said. "We shouldn't put our own feelings first."

Her husband stared at the floor.

"It's the fourth time this week," he said.

Gloomily, the trio trooped upstairs.

"It has come to my attention," said the Headmaster, adjusting his dress, "that books and magazines of the most evil and pernicious kind are circulating in my school."

Four thousand eyes suddenly homed in on him. Even the Upper Sixth, who had been cramming for A-levels with an intensity that had reduced them to wizened wrecks, thumbed open their eyelids and struggled to focus on their leader.

"Biggs of 3b," bellowed the Headmaster, "was found yesterday in the east lavatories, locked alone in a cubicle . . ."

"Alone!" gasped the School.

". . . reading Volume III of the *Children's Encyclopaedia!* Also in his possession were current copies of the *Economist*, *History Today*, and the *Highway Code*. QUIET!" shouted the Headmaster, as several girls began screaming and fainting. An uneasy silence settled. He went on: "I fail utterly to understand, when we have a school library full of the most healthy, wholesome texts—*The Perfumed Garden*, *Maurice The Human Stallion*, *Last Exit To Brooklyn*, *Portnoy's Complaint*, to name only the most boring— I fail utterly to understand why boys and girls should creep off to dark corners and fill their minds with cheap non-educational trash. Mens sana in corpore sano, School, and anyone caught reading Enid Blyton will not be allowed to undress on the forthcoming outing to Epping Forest!"

In the body of the hall, shunned by his nudging classmates, Biggs of 3b began pitifully to whimper.

The next day, Biggs of 3b would not get up. There was no observable sickness, no evidence of fever; it was merely that Biggs of 3b lay on his back, staring fixedly at the ceiling, and moving only when a nervous tic racked his small silent frame.

"What is it?" said his mother.

"Nothing," said Biggs of 3b.

"But it's Thursday," said his mother. "It's a very important day at school, isn't it?"

"Yes," said Biggs of 3b.

His brain shrank. Two periods of compulsory Swedish, then O-level Flagellation until lunch. After lunch there was a seminar in Plastic Rainwear II, a period of Petting, and then Free Expression until home-time. He was paired for Free Expression with Cheryl Gurth, who stood a head taller than Biggs of 3b and could crack walnuts with her knees.

His mother looked at him.

"I'll send a note," she said gently. "I'll say: 'Please excuse Nigel Biggs of 3b on account of a bilious attack and severe nose-bleed and a slight chill.' "

She went out and closed the door. Biggs of 3b smiled for the first time in months, and his hands unclenched, and his tic disappeared. A bird sang, and Biggs of 3b closed his grateful eyes.

He was twelve next birthday, and sick of sex.

Wholesale War

"Pure Hornblower!" cried the Daily
Express, when five Israeli gunboats slipped
their Cherbourg moorings and took off
east. So what else could I do, except go
straight back to my Hornblower and read
between one or two lines?

Horace Hornblum's mother sat in a corner of the mean little
room in Somerset House, and wept, silently.

Horace Hornblum's father sat beside her and stared at the
floor. Occasionally, he would shake his head. Occasionally, he
would sigh.

Horace Hornblum stood patiently at the counter, watching
through the window as the clerk's tatty quill squeaked and
splashed across the Deed Poll form. It stopped. A small blot
spread slowly beneath it.

"Right," said the clerk. "Horace Hornblum, born October
8 1785, present age fifteen, occupation cabin boy."

"Cabin boy!" shrieked his mother. She pressed her sodden
hankie to her eyes and rocked back and forth. "Cabin boy!"

"Golden hands he's got," said his father gloomily. "A
pianist's hands. Or a surgeon's hands."

"Both," said his mother. She blew her nose fiercely. "He
could have been both. Operating by day, by night playing
Bach. With such hands he has to be a cabin boy!"

His father took off his hat, and fanned himself mournfully.

"A fortune on harpsichord lessons," he muttered.

"Can you imagine—" his mother choked on a sob, "can you
imagine what those ropes will do to my baby's hands?"

"Blisters," said his father, "like soup-plates."

"Like footballs," said his mother.

They were silent for a while.

"A violinist, even," said his father, at last.

The clerk came back.

"There you go," he said. He slid a fragment of vellum across the counter. "All official. You are now Mr. Horatio Hornblower."

"*Hornblower*!" shrieked his mother. And fainted.

"See?" shouted his father. "See what you've done? Your own mother!"

The newly-christened Hornblower walked over.

"You bring up children," murmured his mother, and passed out again.

"What did I do?" said Hornblower.

His father's eyes sped upwards, beyond the ceiling.

"What did he do? Only break his mother's heart! Only shame his father's family!" He riveted his eyes into his son's. "To change an honourable name is already bad enough. *But to change to such a name*! You meet people, they'd give their right arm to change their name from Hornblower to Hornblum! Believe me. All right, you want to change your name so what's wrong with Churchill? What's wrong with Twistleton-Wickham-Fiennes? What's wrong with Moncrieff Of That Ilk?"

Hornblower set his jaw.

"They're not sailors' names," he said.

"*Sailors*!" screamed his mother.

They carried her out between them. On the steps, his father turned. In his eyes there was a look of heartrending reasonableness.

"Look," he said. "Sailors get sick, right?"

"Right."

"So be a ship's doctor."

Horatio Hornblower shook his head, and they struggled on against the bitter wind, down to the drizzled Thames.

Tall ships bobbed on the Gravesend tide. Gulls wheeled, men sang at capstans, wagonloads of provisions rattled over the cobbles, bound for a dozen gangplanks.

"Ships' chandlering," said Hornblum, "is a good profession."

"There's a fortune in pemmican," said Mrs. Hornblum. "On biscuits I wouldn't even like to guess. Millions, people are making." She glanced sideways at Hornblower, cannily. "You could buy your own boat, someday."

"Your own *navy*," said Hornblum. "Why work for somebody else? You could declare your own wars. There's a fortune in wars. Look at France. Look at Austria."

"That Attila the Hun," said Mrs. Hornblum, "*There* was a businessman."

Horatio Hornblower fixed his young eyes on the steel horizon, dreaming of squadrons in battle order, hearing far cannon, smelling cordite.

"Too late," he said. "I have already signed on aboard *HMS Victory*."

"I was coming to that," said his father.

"What do you mean?" said Hornblower.

His mother sprang, two-handed, to his head and dragged it to her bosom, dislocating his new periwig.

"As if I'd let my baby, at my breast I held him, go off on some *battleship*!"

"Our own flesh and blood," said his father, "splattered all over the floor."

"Deck," said Hornblower.

His father shot out a short, solid arm and smacked his head.

"Deck, floor, what's the difference? When you're splattered, you're splattered."

"*Don't say such things!*" shrieked Mrs. Hornblum. "Don't talk from splattering!" She turned to her son. "You see what you made your father do? You see what aggravation you bring on your parents? Excitement like this, who knows what can happen? A heart attack, it can bring on. An ulcer."

"A malignant growth," said his father gloomily.

His wife fainted.

"You think I'm joking?" said his father, as they propped her unconscious body against a bollard. "What did Nat Rosenblatt do? Dropped dead. Would I lie? Stone dead from a stroke. And all *he* had was his son wouldn't go into partnership. So what should *I* say? Two strokes I'm entitled to. A ruptured spleen, I shouldn't be surprised. You'd think a boy would show some gratitude, his father arranges for him to sail on the *Schwanz*."

"The what?"

"Don't pretend you never heard from *HMS Schwanz*? Your Uncle Sam's boat, gowns delivered anywhere, also express alterations on board, missing buttons replaced free, special concessions for orders over a gross."

"But I've signed aboard the *Victory*! I want to sail with Nelson."

His mother's eyes snapped open.

"*Nelson*?" she cried. "They shot his arm off! They shot his eye out! You call *that* a living?"

Whereupon she grabbed Horatio Hornblower by the lapel and dragged him off after his disappearing father who, carrying his son's diddybox and chicken (he had asked for a parrot), was rapidly bearing down on the good ship *Schwanz*.

Two days out on the tossing Channel, Horatio Hornblower came to. He lay on his bunk in the spinning gloom, feeling sicker than he had ever felt before. As he groaned, he felt a familiar item touch his lower lip.

"Your own spoon," said a familiar voice. "Brought along special."

Hornblower sat up.

"Mother!" he cried. "What are you—"

"Eat first. Later, you can ask questions. Eat the soup, dolly."

"But I can't have relatives aboard."

"Relatives, relatives! Who's a relative? I'm your *mother*!"

"But a cabin-boy can't have his mother on—"

Soup drowned his sentence.

"From cabin-boys I wouldn't know," said Mrs. Hornblum. "All I know is from my son the captain."

"*Captain*?"

"Your father had a talk with Uncle Sam. It's all arranged. Personally, I wanted admiral for you. Rear-admiral the very

30

least. But your father says it takes time. A whole year, maybe. A lot of people to see, it's not so easy."

"But I don't know how to command a ship!" shrieked Hornblower.

"What's to know? You get a wind, you sail a ship. You don't think your father, from nothing he built a business up, can't drive a lump of wood?"

"Father? Is he here, too?"

Mrs. Hornblum smiled happily, and began cutting up his greens.

"So what else are parents for?" she said.

The Hornblum family stood at the wheel, in the needling sleet. Above them, the canvas creaked; below them, the boards heaved.

"Three times already we passed that rock," shouted Mrs. Hornblum.

"Rubbish!" roared Hornblum above the gale. "To you all rocks look the same."

"Suddenly he knows from rocks!" screamed his wife. "Suddenly we got a rock expert in the family!"

"I think she's right," said Horatio Hornblower.

His father glowered at him from beneath his sou'wester rim.

"Shut up!" he yelled. "Captains should be seen and not heard."

"Yes," said Mrs. Hornblum. "Don't answer your father back. Show a little respect."

"Children!" cried Hornblum. "All they know is to argue."

"You shouldn't even be up here," said Mrs. Hornblum to her son. "A chill on the liver you could get. Triple pneumonia. In both lungs. And who will you expect to nurse you?"

They passed the rock again.

"You go to sea," said Hornblum bitterly, "and what do you get? Heartache."

When the storm finally blew itself out, they saw the ship off the starboard bow, a mile or so away. Three masts, two tiers of cannon, and a French flag.

"Clear the decks!" cried Horatio Hornblower. "Action stations! Man the guns!"

The men looked up from their ironing-boards.

"Don't listen to him!" cried Mrs. Hornblum.

They went on pressing.

Hornblum ran up the Norwegian flag.

"What's that?" cried his son. "What are you doing?"

"Again with the questions!" snapped Hornblum. He lowered a bum-boat and, pulled by four stout trouser-cutters, set a direct course for the French man-o'-war.

They waited. The two ships moaned on their hawsers. Once, an albatross flew overhead, but Mrs. Hornblum shrieked at it, and it planed away westward. After about an hour, Hornblum returned. He was not alone.

The French captain shook hands with everyone. Then, with a small, stiff bow, he handed his sword to Horatio Hornblower.

"What's that for?" demanded Mrs. Hornblum. "An edge like a razor. He could cut himself. Blood-poisoning he could get."

"It's required," said Hornblum, "when you surrender."

"*Surrender*?" cried Horatio Hornblower. "Nobody fired a shot!"

"So who's complaining? Better surrender—"

The French captain held up his hand. They looked at him.

"God forbid I should come between a father and his son," he said, "only do me a favour, don't call it a surrender."

Hornblum nodded.

"How about merger? After all, you're still getting forty-nine per cent of the gross, in return for all the tax-free advantages of my brother-in-law Sam's Panamanian company."

"Merger is better," said the French captain. "Merger I like."

"You think Napoleon will understand?" said Mrs. Hornblum.

The Frenchman gave a short laugh.

"Napoleon!" he said. "So what does a little *schnip* like Napoleon understand from war?"

Ear, Believed Genuine Van Gogh, Hardly Used, What Offers?

"Next Tuesday, Sotheby's are to auction a
lock of Lord Byron's hair." *The Times*

I have a friend in Wells, Somerset, who has a hat belonging to Isambard Kingdom Brunel. Not, of course, as a result of a drunken post-prandial cock-up in some Victorian bistro in which Marx went off with Thackeray's raincoat and Dickens hobbled away in Emily Bronte's gumboots, but because of some astute, or some would say idiot, bidding at an Oxford sale some ten years ago.

The hat stands today on a small davenport in a house belonging to the Abbey National Building Society, whose financial acumen may be said to outstrip that of my friend. However, the hat is more of a talking-point than the house, I'll give him that. It is, indeed, the only object of interest in the place. The first time I saw this moulting felt cylinder, the soft Somerset sunshine highlighting the moth-grubs feasting round its myriad holes, I said, quick as a flash, "What's that?"

Normally, it is only in the cheaper women's magazines that a glint may be said to come into a man's eye. He may also have drawn in his breath with a faint hiss.

"That's Isambard Kingdom Brunel's hat," he said. "He may well have been wearing it when the *Great Eastern* sank."

We looked at it together, as if it bore some tangible sign of engineering history.

"He may," said its new owner, "have taken it off to scratch his head while wondering—"

"—if it was possible to throw an iron bridge across the River Dart?"

"Exactly! Isn't it marvellous?"

In a curious way, I suppose it was. It was concrete evidence that history was more than fiction—few people, I'm sure, *really* believe that men fought one another at Flodden with long sharp swords, without benefit of television, antibiotics, or man-made fibres. One requires three-dimensional resassurance of events that took place before one's grandfather was born; that's what's good about Hampton Court Palace and Shakespeare folios. Here we were, in 1965, looking at Isambard Kingdom Brunel's hat; no surer proof of his existence could have been offered. In its very ordinariness lay its honesty. That is probably why my friend, who has no interest in shipping, ironfounding, or, indeed, I. K. Brunel, bought it.

Of course, there are innumerable reasons why people turn over large wads of negotiable lettuce every day in return for some tatty fragment of arcane reliquiae. This is not to mention museums, whose spies forage the sale-rooms like agents of Dr. Frankenstein, looking for likely bits to enhance their Samuel Johnson house, or Great Plague Of London room, making a jigsaw of time for the benefit of parties of yawning school-children who file past these precious morsels snatched back from mortality and inscribe "Norman Binns Form 3a 1970" on the escritoire at which Castlereagh blew most of his brains out. But museums apart, the list of reasons for which citizens rip out cheques in return for items of no intrinsic value must be endless, from the interior-decorating philistine—"You know what the corner needs to pick up the Regency motif, Mrs. Greebs-Wibley? It needs the Duke of Wellington's bidet, that's what it needs, with a rubber-plant in it, and possibly a nice skull, *comme mémoire du Diable*"—to the intoxicated near-necrophiliac, who sits all day in Che Guevara's socks, weeping for gone glory and decomposing heroes. It may be that the lock of Byron's hair, unsold at the time of going to press, will be knocked down to one such fan, if the University of Texas doesn't get there first, because the God of Romanticism left countless worshippers to pass the bitter-sweet message on to succeeding generations: the old ladies rocking themselves back and forth on chintz upholstery, murmuring cantos of *Don Juan* and imagining themselves taken, firmly but tenderly, on the incense-smelling carpet of Lord B's Venetian bed-sitter, may look more respectable than the teeny-boppers who stuff each new Buddy Holly posthumous LP beneath their pillows, but they're no less potty. If the lock of hair has gone to one of them, it can count itself lucky: it's all velvet cushions and fond kisses from now on. If it's been snapped up by a male fan, it's in for a rougher time, and may well end up sellotaped to his forehead, being regularly tugged for inspiration as he paces back and forth in his carefully ruined Hampstead attic trying to find a rhyme for "mat."

Mind you, it may well have been bought by the time you read this, and if you're still listening, by a spry merchant bank, or Save-And-Prosper Unit Trust, something like that, with an eye to the main chance and a shrewd investment. Who knows what it might fetch in fifty years' time, split up, say, into one-hair lots to avoid the penalty of capital gains? There's always the chance, of course, that Byron may fall from favour and interest, or that the entire opus will turn out to have been written by Isambard Kingdom Brunel and published under an assumed name to avoid accusations of frivolity being levelled at a man who was trying to drum up money for his Channel Tunnel project (which would bang up the value of his hat overnight), but that's the investment game for you. Personally, I'd go a bundle on Byron hair, whatever the *Financial Times* thinks: look at the case of Mahomet—his most Holy Relic is a mere two inches of one beard-hair, over which wars have been fought on a number of occasions. If you'd been wise enough to have bought that during the slack period, in around AD 600 and before he'd made a name for himself, you'd have more than money today. You'd have eight hundred million Muslims ready to follow you anywhere.

And that, friends, is the nub and crux. It's the case of Poseidon shares all over again—the world must be full of citizens kicking themselves for not having snapped up relics when the price was rock-bottom, only to see them soaring through the charts and turning canny paupers to lonely million-aires at the touch of a gavel. Sadly, as with so much else about history's heroes, it's the spotting of potential fame that's the difficulty, whether it's publishing their poems, or hanging their paintings, or buying their old underwear. Think of the great men whose lives passed in penury and hacking coughs due to public unawareness that their littlest possession would one day end up in Sotheby's or the basement of Fort Knox. Imagine poor I. K. Brunel, at the depth of his fortunes after the *Great Eastern* had gone down like a tin brick, rushing into a Burlington Arcade antiquerie with a brown-paper parcel and muttering "Do you a very nice hat, brother, fraught with history, mono-grammed inside, worn throughout the period I was inventing the watertight bulkhead?" What sort of response do you suppose that would have evoked, if not an assistant manger's boot up the backside of a pair of breeches which, had the fool realised it, would today be worth twice as much as the hat? And what of Byron, stuck in the middle of *Childe Harold* and the bailiffs about to carry off his quill? How would he have fared, had he attempted to put his sideburns on the market? Given his reputation at the time, terror of catching something off the precious locks would have had the floorwalkers shrieking for the Bow Street Runners in nought seconds flat, who'd have chucked the shorn bard into a small dark room and thrown the key into the Thames.

Those of you who know me will by now, I think, have cottoned on to this matchless drift. Mine is no mere idle reflec-tion on fame, or hair. Things have been a shade dodgy lately, what with the second instalment of Schedule D for the tax year 72-73 already overdue, and the Inland Revenue poised at the drop of a summons to distrain upon my chattels, so I'd like to let you in on the ground floor. Offer you an unprecedented chance to cash in on what, after the worms sit burping around my supine dust, will be a reputation fit to keep the encyclopae-dia-writers in work for years and force the sale-rooms to take on whole armies of extra staff. Why wait for prices to boom beyond reach? Why fiddle around with building society deposits at five per cent after tax, when you could own a Coren shirt today, actually worn while this article (or, as it will later be known, British Museum MS 68854/ac) was being written, or a *matched pair* of Coren boots, as originally issued to Genuine Naval Officers, but now weighing down the feet of one of the greatest reputations which will ever be made?

The author will be signing vests at Austin Reed, Regent Street, between 10 and 5.30, weekdays only. Don't be late: the first edition is limited to 500 only.

It's Yellow! It's Glittering! It's New! (Fragment)

Every copywriter in every advertising agency has, as you know, a half-finished novel tucked away in his lower left-hand drawer. Unable to resist, I picked a lock, and discovered . . .

. . . first met Emma Bovary at a quiet little soirée thrown by the Strive-Glitterings on the croquet lawn beside the moat of Strive-Glittering Castle. It was an unpretentious affair, just sixty-eight close friends sitting at a long rosewood table, nibbling thin mint chocolates and laughing, while, in the hazy half-distance, golden-haired chauffeurs in tight grey uniforms strolled arrogantly among the moonlit radiators, practising their leers.

Emma was a ravishing woman, married, as I had found out, to a man earning twenty thousand a year, living in Godalming in a house with gas-fired central heating, two cars, a golden retriever, and a four-berth ketch; he took the *Financial Times*, *Yachting World*, and the *Economist*, three holidays a year, and always travelled first class, spending four hundred and thirty pounds p.a. on drinks, and eight hundred on clothes. He smoked small cigars.

It was when she leaned suddenly in front of me, reaching towards the two tiny silver pots and selecting the butter with an accuracy and an assurance that took one's breath away, that I caught a tantalising whiff of her expensive French perfume.

"I just caught," I said, "a tantalising whiff of your expensive French perfume."

She laughed, tinklingly, and the starlight winked on her stain-free teeth.

"I don't use expensive French perfume," she murmured, "in the way you think. But every bar of fabulous pink Camay contains scents made to a special formula by top French parfumiers, exclusively for You. Or, rather, Me. It also contains a cleansing ingredient, a moisture cream, and a thing for keeping gnats off."

"Your skin is like a baby's bum," I said.

She lowered demure eyelids, and fluttered lashes that couldn't have gone out at less than 29/11 the pair.

"You're too gallant," murmured Emma Bovary. "You've noticed I have no unsightly facial hair?"

I nodded.

"Yes," I said, "nor boils, warts, blackheads, acne, barber's rash or moles with bristles on them. Do you use Valderma?"

"Doesn't every girl?" she said, and my blood raced! Inadvertently our warm thighs touched, hesitated, and pressed together.

"I shouldn't be doing this," I whispered.

"It's quite all right," she said, "skirts in the new man-made fibre Finklon will not warp, crease, wither, or ride up. You can even," and her soft voice dropped an octave, quivering, "lie flat in them with complete assurance."

"But your husband?"

"He's on top of a mountain in Calabria," she said, "drinking Dubonnet."

"Way up there?"

"Quite."

Our hands touched, briefly, beneath the cloth.

"Convincing tests have shown," I said, "that four out of every five women would rather go home with me than sit around waiting for their husbands to come in and distinguish between different types of instant mashed potato."

"Incredible!"

"Not incredible," I said, "*biological*."

We eased our chairs back, and stood up; but before we could leave, our hostess, the Hon. Fenella Strive-Glittering, shimmered across the dewy grass with a young Apollo on either arm.

"Emma!" she cried. "Leave Nigel here! I'm prepared to offer not just one, but *two* young men in exchange for the one you've got there!"

Emma shook her lovely wig.

"No, thanks very much, I'll stick to my Nigel."

Fenella smiled, and shrugged.

"We find that most women do," she said. "And to think that only last year you had halitosis and forty square feet of clear water every time you got into a swimming-pool!"

"It's amazing what a ring of confidence will do for a girl," said Emma, "especially if her haemorrhoids have been shrunk without painful surgery."

We all smiled, and shook hands, and Emma and I strolled off through the shrubbery. She had removed her shoes, and swung them in her left hand, clasping mine with her right, and leaning her head against the shoulder of my dinner-jacket. My heart pumped madly! Nothing acts faster than adrenalin.

"Is this your car?" she said admiringly, lifting her skirt as she got in and allowing her firm bare leg to set off the mock-lizard, near-leatherette upholstery that comes as standard, together with two-speed wipers, cool-air ventilation, fully reclining seats, walnuteen dashboard, and many other built-in features only obtainable as extras on cars costing hundreds of pounds more.

"Yes," I said, as she ran her hand up the gear-shift and bit into a Cadbury's Flake, "I find it outperforms many a sports car while offering limousine-style comfort for five six-feet adults. Heads turn when I drive by."

"How fortunate, then, that ugly dandruff is not interfering with *your* chance of happiness!" cried Emma.

We got away. In my headlights, cats leapt, and owls watched us, and the dashboard glow picked up Emma's matchless embonpoint, thrusting deliciously forward, thanks to cross-your-heart straps, designed to lift and separate, that were doing a job which even I could not have improved upon. Happily, I reflected that for me, at five-feet-ten and twenty-nine, a worth-while career awaited in today's Metropolitan Police, should I ever need it. It was then that I noticed the two headlamps in my driving-mirror.

"I think we're being followed," I said.

She twisted round.

"You're right!" she cried. "It's a white car, identical to this. Is it merely Paddy Hopkirk testing some new silicone wax polish . . . ?"

"Or your husband, back from his mountain-top, thanks to the unparalleled efficiency and friendly but unobtrusive service which travellers have come to expect from BEA?"

"It cannot be! Tomorrow he is expected off Corfu, drinking tonic water aboard an ocean-going yacht."

I pressed my Corfam slipper to the floor, and we snaked through the wooded lanes at breakneck speed, thankful alike for Pirelli Cinturatos, Milk of Magnesia, Britax Seat Belts, and Mum Aerosol Deodorant, with the white car barely a furlong behind, and gaining. I had all but resigned myself to discovery and disaster, when the delicious Emma glanced over her shoulder, and cried:

"The white car is stopping!"

I looked in my mirror.

"Thank God for the mileage ingredient!" I shouted.

"You mean?"

"Yes! Our red car will continue for another seven-point-two miles, while the poor sod behind is about to end up as just another case of lupine indigestion, if the rising tide doesn't get him first!"

We did not need to drive even that far: mere minutes later, following Emma's directions, we turned down a narrow track and ended up in front of a splendid neo-Georgian house.

"Is this where you live?" I asked.

"Yes," she said. "Fully detached, on two floors only, and with matchless views over the Green Belt, facing south, and a stone's throw from schools, shops, and choice of two stations into London, less than twenty-five minutes away. It is, of course, double-glazed, with a mature yet easily managed garden, and the gazebo lights up at night. It was designed for an elderly lady of title, who built it very very slowly and only used it at weekends. Shall we go in?"

"What about your children?" I whispered.

"These cold mornings," said Emma, "I make sure they don't go out without a good hot breakfast of Weetabix inside them. Its nourishing goodness lasts the whole day through, and keeps rickets away."

"I meant," I said, as she slid the key into the lock, "won't they hear us?"

"No. They're away at their Auntie Eth's. On an egg holiday."

I followed her into the dark hall, the atmosphere heavy with the intoxicating musk of Air-Wick, and was about to sink my teeth into the fleshy luminescence of her gorgeous neck when something large and black sprang through a shaft of moonlight and hurled itself upon me with a fearful noise. As I fell backwards, I caught the unmistakable whiff of marrow-bone jelly.

"Good heavens, Bovary!" I cried, never a man to lose my cool, thanks to my training with the Runcorn Correspondence School of Pelmanism, which made me a mental wizard in only three short weeks, "There's no need to lose your temper, I only dropped in to read the meter and inquire whether you wished to earn money with your pen this winter! I am a Pakistani immigrant, sir, working my way through college, and these magazines—"

"Oh do shut up, Nigel!" exclaimed Emma. "It's only Prince Osric of Hernia III, Champion of Champions. You wouldn't happen to have a tin of Pal about your person?"

"No!" I snapped, as the dog walked away to practise posing.

"Top breeders use it," said Emma reproachfully.

I got to my feet, thankful for the creaseproof qualities of Crimplene, and took her delectable elbow in my palm.

"A top breeder I may be," I said smoothly, "but I do not engage upon the activity on the lower floors. Where is your staircase?"

I felt her tremble.

"Would you not rather ride with me in the moonlight, Nigel? We have two white horses, you know. We could smoke mentholated cigarettes and let the wind blow through our hair."

"Afterwards," I breathed, wedging the Polo against an upper bicuspid with a practised tongue and limbering my freshly salved lips.

"But would you not like to watch our Timmy select Katto-meat from not less than five bowls of assorted horse-offal? Will you not come and drop blood-stained garments in the Hoover-matic? Don't you want to see my budgies bounce with health?"

It was this last wild, provocative question that sent my temples into a mad throb of uncontrollable passion! Popping an Iron Jelloid in my mouth, I snatched the luscious Emma into my arms and took the stairs (thank you, Phyllosan!) three at a time, on the run. But—dear Lord, do words exist to limn the agony of what followed!—it was in that dark, desired boudoir that the revelation occurred so harrowing in its extent, so traumatic in its implications, so . . .

Shrieking her small, impassioned shrieks, Emma Bovary began to fumble out of her clothes. First, the sweet Sheerline tights, Designed To Make Your Legs Even Longer, Even Shapelier—these cast aside, her legs suddenly became even shorter, even lumpier; then the Playtex girdle, whose Fingertip Panels Hold You In Like Firm Young Muscles To Make You Look Five Pounds Thinner, fell to the floor, making her look five pounds fatter and free from all muscletone, like an ill-knit haggis; and when the bra joined the pile, its cross-your-heart straps gone and leaving a bosom lowered and joined, the de-composing Venus stood before me in the pallid moonlight, rapidly balding with the removal of her assorted hair-pieces, her excitement breaking the porcelain maquillage and sending it running down her face in multicolour rivulets.

As her dentures fell, hissing, into the Steradent, Emma Bovary advanced upon me, snapping at my outstretched hands with her hungry gums, and, before I could . . .

Oh Why Was It Built So Beautiful?
Why Was It Built At All?

"The London Region Group of the Royal
Institute of British Architects is asking
anyone who thinks they have spotted a
masterpiece built between 1914 and 1950
to let them know." *Evening Standard*

The London Region Group,
RIBA,
Portland Place,
London, W1.

Gentlemen:

May I first of all say, on behalf of the twenty million or so
souls currently inhabiting the architectural gems so lovingly set
in this island shank over the past fifty years, how thrilled and
delighted we are at your interest in these masterpieces that have
lain so long neglected by connoisseurs and demolition contrac-
tors alike? For those of us who believe that the period represents
a Golden Age in English structural aesthetics beside which
St. Paul's and Canterbury are the mere bricky gropings of
untutored primitives, keeping the faith has not always been
easy. While fawning sentimentalists and gullible sycophants
rush shrilling to each surviving fragment of Nash terrace and
spotty Jones portico, while ten thousand tourist shutters clack
in the face of any mouldering Georgian error, while charabanc-
loads of Colour Supplement hacks tumble out, typing, before
some newly threatened Victorian pissoir, the eternally lovely
objects of our taste have had reserved to them only the world's

derision. When was the last time that Thos. Cook ushered a rapt party of Japs down Lewisham High Road, or carried tradition-slavering Americans out to the garages of Potters Bar and Cockfosters Tube Station? When was the last roll of Koda-chrome expended on the stone nuances of the British Home Stores, Kilburn, or that lovely thing that so deftly masks the cliché of St. Paul's from strollers breasting Ludgate Hill? And among the fat, sweet-smelling pile of coffee-table gloss so keenly packaged each season by Britain's swinging publishers, where is Nigel Nicolson's *Great English Launderettes*, James Morris's *Wembley*, or Sir Kenneth Clark's *Bus Shelter Symposium*?

No doubt you have by now been inundated with snapshots, bricks, and data by all those spotters who, like me, have been waiting only for the first trickle to spurt through the great flood-gates of taste. Other lovers of London and its heritage will already have drawn your attention to the nestling villages of asbestos prefabs still to be seen in most of our boroughs, those imperishable examples of inspired thought and craftsmanship tucked away behind their delicate tracery of chicken-wire fencing, rusting now with soft antiquity, girt with the sculpted corrugation of outside loos and sinking into ever more attractive poses, thanks to the care that went into refusing to install foundations. They were, of course, designed to be pulled down by 1950, but were mercifully preserved by the devoted hand of succeeding Housing Ministers. God, truly, is not mocked! Other cognoscenti, I am convinced, will have pointed out the masonic wonders of the Gaumont chain, the early 'fifties council estates with their identical midget windows, ribbed glass doors and gravelled playgrounds, the sweet exquisitries of Heathrow Airport and the Financial Times Building, at which architects from all over the civilised world have come to stare and wonder, the London Hilton with its matchless views of Knightsbridge Barracks and the Shell Building . . . the list is endless. I myself could dwell forever on the concept of the semi, that Grand Design that sums up all that British domestic architecture meant between the wars, those superb twinnings so bravely refusing to be one thing or another, often with

45

detached garages tacked wittily to their sides and garnished with lemon stucco or the sporadic beauty of rough-cast and wrought-iron gate, proudly holding their serried and indistinguishable ranks for mile upon mile of Crescent, Avenue, and Lane.

Does anywhere else in the world have neo-Tudor residences? Can any foreign citizen put his hand upon his heart and say: "Yes, we too produced two million mullioned windows in 1934"? Were Edgware on a lake, would Venice survive another summer season?

But these are accepted generalities, and known truths, and my purpose in writing to you today is not to catalogue glories available to anyone blessed with a taste for outside guttering and pre-cast ingle-nooks. You ask, specifically, if anyone has spotted a masterpiece built during the period, and I answer, confidently. Yes. I am, in fact, penning this submission from inside the masterpiece in question at this very moment; any flakes of plaster that find their way into the envelope should be returned to the above address, where they will be treated with the respect due to a fabric so delicate that a thousand words banged out on an Olivetti can leave a room stripped to its joists and wiring.

The house itself was built a few years ago by undoubted experts, possibly a brain surgeon and a lepidopterist, and passed into my hands through a happy accident, my bank having failed to stop the cheque in time; the amount involved would have been enough to have packed the Sistine Chapel aboard three trucks and shipped it to Disneyland for reassembly, so you can see that this is no mean property. Despite outward appearances. Though but a decade old, it is rapidly assuming all the rich photogenic characteristics of venerated antiquity, and has, in my humble opinion, already outstripped Anne Hathaway's Cottage and is well on the way to giving York Minster a run for its money. By 1980 or thereabouts, I fully expect Stonehenge to be a back number, as flocks of tourists and antiquarians turn their backs on Salisbury Plain in favour of poking among the rubble around my bed and questioning one another as to its possible religious significance.

Constructed entirely of a brick which has now, sadly, gone out of production, due, no doubt, to new processes which have shown that the same item can be produced more cheaply by mixing sand and sea-water in a child's plastic bucket, the house was built on the site of what was probably a famous old Hole. Though builder's rubbish, twigs, old pottery, bits of galvanised pail, and several small four-legged skeletons were used to fill it in, parts of the original Hole may still be seen by the simple process of walking onto the terrace at the point where it is moving gradually away from the house towards what used to be called the garden. It may be, of course, that it is the house which is moving away from the terrace, as the man next door claims, but there may well be other reasons why his garage is being nudged downhill, and I do not pretend to be an expert on itinerant brick.

Shouldering aside the trusty three-ply door and replacing the relevant jambs, we find ourselves only a stride away from the rear garden, a fascinating trompe d'oeil achieved by making the ground floor as small as possible. On our left, one of the few dining-rooms in London where a married couple has to eat in shifts, on our right, a kitchen that could be described as the ultimate in labour-saving economy, impossible as it is to open even a can of beans without first placing one elbow in the garden and one foot in the sink. These two rooms are cunningly connected by a hatch which can be jemmied open in a matter of minutes, enabling anyone trapped in the dining-room by the wedged door to lean through and bang his head on the fridge.

It was a security-conscious hand indeed that carpentered the stairs: not only does the slightest tread on any one of them call up a noise piquantly redolent of an elderly yew-tree falling beneath the axe, but they will also perform this endearing trick quite spontaneously, usually during the small hours, forcing the householder to take much-needed exercise in the middle of some profitless and debilitating dream. Expert opinion has attributed this to the wisdom and foresight of installing central heating in an environment of sodden and unseasoned wood, a trick that only very few civil engineers have ever got the hang of, and one which also relieves the busy occupant of the bother of trying to open and close windows. Many a night and oft have I lain, unable to sleep, lulled by the pleasing noise of the plumbing talking to the carpentry, interrupted by the witty asides of the tiles dropping off the roof and shattering upon the brown lawns beneath. (No space, here, to write of the spacious gardens themselves, landscaped around their central motif—the largest willow-stump in the western hemisphere—by the previous occupant's horticultural staff of, I believe, goats.)

Had I more time and space, I should expatiate on the virtue of the integral garage, which has proved to be the only successful method of introducing petrol fumes into the bedrooms on the upper floors, or the two bathrooms which have done so much to prevent the ceilings beneath them from remaining so boringly level and monochromatic, or the taps which come off so readily in the hand and make delightful conversation pieces for guests breaking their way back into the living room after an hour's refreshing wrestling in the closets. But why go on? I do most sincerely trust that you will hurl aside whatever trivial business is currently clogging your desks, gentlemen, and hurry on down. Believe me, my house is yours.

For a small consideration, used notes only please.

It's A Long Way To Cannelloni

"The British soldier is becoming a
gourmet. To wartime soldiers brought up
on bully beef stew, the Catering Corps
cookery book would seem unbelievable. It
contains 1,076 recipes. But their resources
will be tested to the full next week, with the
arrival in Aldershot of shooting teams
from all over the world for the Central
Treaty Organisation Small Arms Shooting
Competition." *Sunday Telegraph*

In the dank dug-out, one candle flickered. The heavy air reeked
of fatigue and soaked serge and garlic and saltimbocca alla
romana. Above, along the old duckboards, old ducks went up
the line to death, to be stuffed, spitted, sauced, and then forgotten. There had been some talk at Base of raising a memorial
to the Unknown Duck, when it was all over, but it would be a
long time before that day came. In the no-man's-land between
the clattering mobile canteens and the rat-tat-tat of the Ken-
wood .303 foodmixers, young pigs squealed horribly, and died.
The awful stink of burning flesh was everywhere.

At a makeshift chopping-table, Captain Stanhope sat over
his cookery book, ball-point poised. It wasn't easy to find the
right words. Taramasalata, had the brigadier said? Or was it
tarragon? Or tagliatelle? They had all been out here too long.
Stanhope's eyes were ringed with dark shadows from too much
stuffing; his fingers were scored from dicing with carrots; his
hair was falling out.

Sergeant Trotter, who had been there and back, and there
again, and seen it all, who had done the porridge at Alamein

and smoked the haddocks for the Imjin River brunches, came down the rickety stairs, slopping an enamel mug. He put it on Stanhope's table.

"Go on, sir," he said. "Get that inside you."

Stanhope sipped the fragrant skate-liver-and-jasmine broth.

"He should have been back by now, Trotter."

"You can't never tell, sir. It's no good thinking the worst. Every cloud has a silver lining."

"Good old Trotter!" Stanhope, despite the heaviness breeding about his heart, laughed the brave young laugh that had carried him through so much, through a hundred collapsed soufflés and a thousand curdled bortschs. Stanhope had seen many flies in many soups. "Good old Trotter, you always know the right thing to say!"

"An apple a day keeps the doctor away, sir."

"God knows that's true, Trotter."

"Persil washes whiter, sir."

Stanhope sighed and nodded.

"Young Raleigh's a child, Trotter. He's only been with us two weeks. He doesn't have the experience. He doesn't have the nerves. They're sending them to us straight from domestic science school, Trotter."

"He'll make out, sir. He's got an old head on young shoulders, has Mr. Raleigh. A stitch in time saves nine, sir."

"I suppose you're right, Trotter. But he's never tackled more than a bread-and-butter pudding, or an apple crumble—and now he's out there facing the Turks with nothing more than a teenage sauce corporal and a few green private can-openers to help him. The Turks'll make mincemeat of them!"

"I had a recipe for human mincemeat once, sir," murmured Trotter, "it's not so bad. Don't you fret, sir. Many a mickle makes a muckle."

Erratic bootsteps thundered overhead, amid weak, sporadic cheering. Stanhope leapt up. As he did so, a fresh-faced youth burst through the doorway, his chef's hat awry and ketchup-stained, and flung himself into the dug-out.

"Raleigh!" cried Stanhope. "Thank God you're safe!"

The young lieutenant wiped his gravied hands on his apron. He looked hard into Stanhope's addled grey eyes.

"It's sheer bloody hell out there, sir!" he cried. "The Turks have broken through our fish pie and it's only a matter of minutes before they begin mopping up."

"God, they're filthy eaters!" muttered Stanhope.

"Give 'em a taste of cold veal!" cried Trotter. "He can't face cold veal, can't Johnny Turk!"

"What about our left flank, old chap?"

"Dreadful, sir," said Raleigh. "Complete bloody shambles. The French are chucking everything they can think of at us—seventy-three orders of tête de veau vinaigrette, forty-eight entrecôtes de quatre saisons, including seventeen saignants, twenty-two bleu, nineteen without parsley, six with rosemary but no thyme, twelve with thyme but no basil, and nobody wants chips. My men are beginning to crack, sir. And I'm afraid the German assault on the knackwurst is beginning to tell—if the sauerkraut gives out, it's going to be impossible to hold them!"

"Dear God!" shouted Stanhope, "It's started earlier than anyone anticipated!"

"You mean—?"

Stanhope hurled his ladle aside.

"Yes, Raleigh, it's the Big Push! And only this morning I had a dispatch rider up from Base saying that Intelligence reckoned we could hold 'em off with two-eggs-chips-sausage-and-beans for at least a week."

"What do they know at Base?" shrieked Raleigh, his slim frame trembling, "sitting around in their shiny kitchens, surrounded by clean Formica and remote-control cookers and waste-disposal units, making one another zabaglione and matelote de brochet au vin rosé? How long is it since any of them was out here, trying to prise the eye out of a sheep for a tableful of Iranian brass who'd have your leg for an hors d'oeuvres as soon as look at you?"

"Steady, old chap!" Stanhope's firm hand came down on Raleigh's lonely pip. Suddenly, an inhuman shriek rocked the dug-out, and a wild-eyed figure sprang through the Habitat beads, waving a Webley. He was dressed in a black tailcoat and a long white apron.

"It's Frobisher!" hissed Stanhope. "He's blown his top!"

"It's the waiting!" screamed Frobisher. "I can't stand it any more!"

"The waiting's always the worst, sir," said Trotter soothingly.

"Seven tables!" howled Frobisher, searching desperately for the trigger, "Two Spanish, two Greek, two Italian, and some madman sitting under the stairs who says he's from the IRA and if I don't bring him a plate of potatoes on the double he'll pull the pin and blow the entire canteen to bits."

"You've just been out here too long, old man," said Stanhope. "We all have."

"None of you has been what I've been through!" sobbed Frobisher. "You forget I'm only seconded to the 17th/21st Entrées. I came from the Queen's Own Yorkshire Light Sommeliers. We were a class mob, we could sniff a '47 Margaux from fifty paces, we could tell a Krug from a Bollinger with our gasmasks on, and there was always a half-bottle or two left over to slip up your pinny after they blew Last Post." His voice broke. "I'll teach those bastards at Command! What's a bloody bullet look like, for God's sake?" He poked frenziedly in the chamber with his corkscrew, sobbing and shaking. "I can't take any more!"

Stanhope drew Raleigh aside.

"I think it's an old omelette wound he sustained at the Royal Tournament," he muttered, "when we were trying to do a fines herbes against the clock. Never been the same since. I'd better get that thing away from him." He set his splendid jaw, reached quickly inside his battledress, and took out a small blue envelope. "Look, I wrote this to Molly when the first hors d'oeuvres started. It's my own recipe for gefilte fish au poivre. If anything happens to me, Raleigh, I'd like you to—"

Suddenly, with a frightful culinary oath, Frobisher hurled the gun aside.

"Useless bloody thing!" he shrieked. He wheeled, and sprang for the stairs. "It's quicker this way!"

"After him, Trotter!" cried Stanhope. "He's making straight for the Dutch front tables, and you know what their appetite's like—they'll have an apple in his gob and a litre of sauce béarnaise running over his back before you can say Regulo Four!"

But it was not to be! An instant later, before even Trotter could unsheathe his trusty carvers, a weird and terrible multilingual din shook the dug-out and filled the gloom with unanswerable questions. Together, unhesitating, Stanhope and Raleigh leapt through the curtain, sprinted for the nearest dessert trench, and hurled themselves in. The air was full of flying onion rings and gnocchi, and prunes were everywhere. Gingerly, they pulled themselves up, and peered over the top. In time to see the khaki backsides of a dozen foreign regiments hurtling for the far horizon, the scattered victuals congealing in their wake.

"Dear Heavens!" cried Raleigh. "It's a bloody rout!"

"What happened?" shouted Stanhope. "What happened?"

A flying figure leapt the rim, and crashed beside them.

"Potter, sir, Sergeant I/C Soups and Cold Appetizers, it was Frobisher, sir, come on like a thing possessed, we couldn't stop him, sir. Before we knew what was happening, he was serving the French up hamburger waffles with jello, he was dishing out squid cous-cous to the Americans, he was hitting the Israelis with ham salads, he was serving haggis to the Dutch and raw roast beef to the Indians—I never seen nothing like it, sir, I never seen hard men break and run. I never seen commandos vomit."

A tear welled up and flashed in Stanhope's eye.

"Gentlemen in England now a-bed," he murmured, "shall think themselves accursed they were not here, Raleigh."

"Will he get a gong, sir?"

"Two, I shouldn't wonder," said Stanhope. "Lunch and dinner. He's saved the Catering Corps, Raleigh. Look at that!"

The broken foreigners had stopped, had turned, were shuffling humbly back. In the silence, bellies rumbled, like far guns.

"Raleigh lad," said Stanhope, "order up two hundred cheese omelettes, and never mind about the rinds. I think our guests are just about ready for their lunch."

And Though They Do Their Best To Bring Me Aggravation . . .

"Did you bring back something special from your holiday? Why not enter our Grand Souvenir Competition?"   *Daily Telegraph*

When Sir Henry Souvenir (1526-1587) at last returned to the court of Queen Elizabeth from his ten-year tour of the Orient, he little thought that their opening exchange would pass into history.

"What have you brought for me?" asked his queen.

"It's a box made from the liver of an elephant, your majesty," replied Sir Henry, "wrought in strange fashion by the natives and covered in sea-shells. You can keep fags in it."

"Where did you get it?" she inquired.

"I can't remember," he said.

And thus it was that the pattern of the next four hundred years was firmly laid. Ever since that fateful day in 1570, people have been coming back from distant parts carrying things to put cigarettes in, which they give to other people to remind them of places that neither of them can recall. The word "souvenir" has, of course, slightly extended itself in meaning until it now denotes almost anything either breakable or useless; but even today, ninety per cent of the items covered by the word are forgettable objects in which cigarettes can be left to go stale.

Some people don't actually give their souvenirs away, preferring instead to build up a vast collection with which to decorate lofts; it is not immediately clear why they do this, but a strong ritualistic element is clearly involved, no doubt because the objects are themselves closely associated with the passing of time and take on a totemistic quality from this association. Souvenirs, for example, can never be thrown away, probably because to do so would be to wipe out the past of which they are the only extant record. They are, however, moved around the loft every five years or so, when their lids tend to fall off or, in the case of clocks, when their cuckoos fall out.

The cuckoo clock, in fact, may be said to be the quintessential souvenir, in that it exists purely to be bought, sold, wrapped, carried home, unwrapped, and put in lofts. It never hangs on walls. It is usually purchased in Switzerland, where it never hangs on walls either. How it became involved with Switzerland is a horological mystery of a high order, but experts have suggested that since Switzerland has nothing else to identify it (i.e., Eiffel Towers, Taj Mahals, castanets, lederhosen, chopsticks), and since both its national products, snow and chocolate, melt, the cuckoo clock was invented solely in order to give tourists something solid to remember it by. The undeniable success of the cuckoo clock has led the Swiss to branch out with typically cautious adventurousness: removing the tiny house from which the cuckoo emerges, they have enlarged it in recent years and inserted a music-box inside it, which, when you lift the lid, starts to play "O Mine Papa" and breaks.

It's for keeping cigarettes in.

Mention of the Eiffel Tower and the Taj Mahal lead me naturally to point out an important secondary characteristic of the souvenir. It is invariably an imitation of something else. Even when it's original. Inventiveness of a remarkable kind often goes into this imitation, and accusations of vulgarity by citizens like Lord Snowdon (who has himself been called a vulgar imitation, though not by me) do not detract from the brilliance of the minds that, for example, saw in the Eiffel Tower not a thousand feet of iron, but six inches of salt-cellar with a nude in the base and a thermometer up one side. Not that our own English craftsmen have been left behind in the race for international kudos: a mere mile from where I am writing this, you can buy a midget guardsman with ten fags in his busby and a gas lighter on his rifle, or a pygmy beefeater out of whose cunningly constructed mouth twenty different scenes of London may be pulled, in full colour. All over Kansas, at this very moment, recent visitors to Britain will be trying to glue its head back on.

Souvenirs also have an invaluable role to play as conversation pieces, even though there will usually be more pieces than conversation. The talk is often quite fascinating, viz:

"Yes, we bought that in Brussels, ha-ha-ha, amusing isn't it? When you switch it on, it pees. Oh. Well, it did. Perhaps it needs a new batt— now look what you've done, it's come off in your hand. We'll never get the cigarettes out of it now." Or;

"This nut-dish is constructed entirely out of a single piece of elkhorn, by the way, and the crackers are made from the ribs of an okapi. Yes. O-K-A-P-I. And now, if you care to pick up that pin-cushion in the shape of the Great Pyramid, you will find— oh, really? But it's only nine o'clock, and of course you haven't even seen our Nefertiti door-step yet, THAT CARPET YOU'RE RUNNING DOWN IS AN EXTREMELY FASCINATING EXAMPLE OF VERY EARLY SUDANESE . . ."

It's not always easy to choose souvenirs, of course, and many people swear by clothes. I myself have sworn by a suit I bought in Hong Kong some years ago, and hope one day to bring out the oaths in book form, as soon as permissiveness establishes itself a little more securely. As everyone knows, Hong Kong has some of the finest tailors in the world, but what they actually do there is open to question, since all the clothes are made by some of the worst. My own suit, hacked from a wonderfully dirt-absorbent length of, I think, Kleenex, is loosely piled on the floor of the loft, being unable to stay on its hanger. It was, of course, cheap—less than four times as much as a similar article picked up in Savile Row when, due to a light shower in Piccadilly, the Hong Kong item started gripping my flesh with all the enthusiasm of an under-nourished vampire—and this probably accounts for the way in which it was cut, since malformed Oriental dwarfs do not, I'm sure, carry much ready cash upon their persons. It's a wonderful conversation-piece, mind. People I'd known intimately for years suddenly began pointing out that they'd never realised I had one shoulder five inches lower than the other or that my inside leg measured fourteen inches. Osteopaths would approach me in the street and offer their services free in the interest of science.

Not that I'll be entering it in the *Telegraph* competition, though. The suit has competition enough at home, and my initial problem is selecting exactly which rare and precious item to blow the dust off in order to pick up the six quid with which the *Telegraph* hopes to console me for the misspent years of haggling in bazaars and dragging crates through airports and lashing out enough customs dues to turn the *real* Arc de Triomphe into a musical needlework cabinet and knock the bottom out of the French souvenir trade for ever. What shall I choose from the matchless hoard? The genuine Matabele shield, riddled with moth-holes? (No wonder Rhodesia is run by a white minority, if that's all there was between the natives and the Maxim gun.) The elephant's foot wastebasket, perhaps the most macabre thing ever to pass across a counter? (When we came home from India and unwrapped it, the toenails fell off.) The solid brass table-top we bought at the same Delhi shop which peeled on the plane, and rusted in the cab back from Heathrow? The hand-sewn slippers from Alexandria which gave rise to a condition which has baffled chiropodists throughout the civilised world? My genuine Dutch meerschaum, that glows in the dark, blisters, and flakes off on to the authentic Bokhara rug which is supposed to have taken two generations of Uzbeks to weave and which it took the cat one evening to unravel?

On second thoughts, I don't think I'll bother. Let someone else take the *Telegraph*'s money with his walrus-tooth-letter-opener-barometer-and-shoehorn combined, I'm hanging on to my stock. Some day soon, the Martian package tourists are going to start arriving, and I'm going to be down there at the saucerport handing out my copper-plate business cards.

Give 'em a free glass of mint tea, and those people'll buy anything.

Go Easy, Mr Beethoven, That Was Your Fifth!

"Shrunk to half its proper size, leathery in consistency and greenish-blue in colour, with bean-sized nodules on its surface." Yes, readers, I am of course describing Ludwig van Beethoven's liver, and I do apologise for going over such familiar ground, but I wanted to put the less musical members of my flock in the picture right from the start. I think they also ought to know that his spleen was more than double its proper size: far too many *soi-disant* music-lovers these days, when they drop the pick-up on *Egmont* or the *Eroica* and retire to their chaise longue for a quick listen, think to themselves *Poor old sod, he was deaf as a brick*, and leave it at that, entirely neglecting the fact that beneath the deaf-aid on his waistcoat Herr van Beethoven sported as misshapen a collection of offal as you could shake a stick at, including a pancreas the size of a pickled walnut and a length of intestine that could have been mistaken for pipe-lagging by all but the most astute German plumber.

I am reminded of all this internal strife by today's *Guardian*, which, in its copy-hungry turn, quotes from the current issue of the *Journal of Alcoholism*, a periodical of which I had not previously heard. Which is odd, since if I'm not on their mailing-list, who is? At all events, this bizarre broadsheet has clearly decided that it is not going to be outdone in Ludwig's bicentenary year by all the other mags, and has hopped aboard the wagon, if they'll pardon the expression, with a succinct length of verbiage by one Doctor Madden, consultant psychiatrist at a Chester hospital addiction unit. He it is whom I quote at the beginning of this *feuilleton*, and if I may say so, Doctor, as one

59

stylist to another, I have rarely encountered so well-turned a memorial to a great man. Why that sentence was not chiselled on Ludwig van Beethoven's gravestone, I shall never know. I gather you've translated it from the report of his autopsy, and it may be that it reads even better in German, but I doubt it: poetry is what "bean-sized nodule" is, and don't let anyone tell you otherwise. Indeed, you may well have altered the listening habits of an entire generation: how shall any of us be able to tune in to *Fidelio* again, without the tears springing to our eyes at the memory of the greenish-blue liver behind it? Will our rapture at the *Emperor* not be intensified beyond measure by the thought of that gigantic spleen, throbbing away like a ship's boiler under the composer's vest?

One flaw, however, mars the sunny scholarship of your piece: not content to commemorate the bicentenary merely by your thrilling evocation of distorted bowel and giblet and leaving it at that, you insist, I'm afraid, on going on to moralise. And it's none of your business, Doc. Having broken the unethical news that Ludwig's organs got this way through a daily consumption of booze that could have floated a Steinway down Kaiserstrasse, you then wind up the scoop with the homiletic clincher: "Beethoven had a brain and mind capable of many years of musical productivity, had his life not been shortened by alcohol." Now, I realise that this oleaginous aside may have been the result of editorial pressure, and that if you hadn't put it in all your readers might have rushed out immediately and begun hitting the sauce in the hope of coming up with a quartet or two, but couldn't you have turned the sentiment a little less harshly? And aren't you being just a teeny bit demanding? Aren't nine symphonies, thirty-two piano sonatas, seven concertos, two masses, sixteen string quartets, and two suit-casefuls of quintets enough for you and the rest of mankind?

And don't you perhaps feel that, after that lot, posterity owes Ludwig a little snort or two?

I suppose not. All human life is divided between those who order by the crate and those who believe that sherry trifle leads to the everlasting bonfire, and never the twain shall meet except

on the sodden salient of the *Journal of Alcoholism* for such brief
and bitter skirmishes as the one filleted above. You're on one
side, Doc, and Ludwig and I are on the other. My own con-
clusion would be diametrically different from yours, viz, that if
Beethoven had *not* been a regular supplier of empties to the
trade, he wouldn't have written anything at all, and how does
that grab you, abstemious musicologists? If the great man had
been confined to Lucozade on the advice of Chester's addiction
unit, my bet is that he'd have thrown in the towel at *Chopsticks*
and gone down in history as a mediocre hosier.

Because it is no accident that all men of creative genius have
toiled in the shadow of the corkscrew—how else is a giant to
survive among pygmies, make the mundane tolerable, fence
himself off from the encroachments of numbing normalcy?
How but through regular intakes of fermented anaesthetic are
we—there, I've said it—artists to stave off the canvas jacket and
the screaming abdab? How must Beethoven have felt of a
morning, his head full of whirling crotchets and jangling semi-
breves, to have his housekeeper running off at the gob about
the price of vermicelli, or shrieking through his blessed deafness
in an attempt to bring home to him the immutable truth that
if you send six pillow-cases to the laundry, you only ever get
five back? Is it any wonder that he followed up his Special K
with a few quick chasers of schnapps? Do you for one moment
imagine that the Piano Concerto No. 4 in G Major was written
by a teetotaller, given the fact that the decorators were in the
haus at the time, Beethoven's shoes hadn't come back from the
cobblers, he was four months overdue on his Schedule D pay-
ment, his mistress had run off with a door-to-door wurst salesman, and the dog had just trodden on his glasses?

And, worst of all, people like you, Doctor Madden, were
constantly nagging him to get on with the bloody music, what
about a couple of quick symphonies to follow up the 9th,
shouldn't take you more than an hour or so to rattle 'em off,
mate, and how would you like to address the Rotarians next
Wednesday night, dress formal, and isn't it time you did a
personal tour of Silesia, and by the way it's the Prime Minister's

birthday coming up, so could you see your way clear to knocking out a little celebratory sextet, no fee naturally, oh yes, I nearly forgot, my wife's brother plays the triangle, not professional of course, but we all think he's rather good, so I've arranged a little dinner-party next Friday to give you the chance of hearing him . . .

I'm amazed his nodules didn't get any bigger than beans, all things considered.

It's a dodgy tightrope along which we creators wobble, Doc: enough booze to close the world off and keep us inventing, but not so much that we allow the golden haze to settle on us permanently, while the piano-strings slacken, and the typewriter rusts, and the brushes dry out and go stiff, and the public yawns and goes off in search of fresh fodder, muttering about what an inconsiderate bleeder that Shakespeare was, snuffing it in his fifties and leaving us with little more than *Lear*, *Hamlet*, *Macbeth*, *Othello*, *Anthony and Cleopatra*, well I'm not surprised, you know what they say, he couldn't leave the stuff alone, liver like a dried pea, well that's the trouble with artists, isn't it, hoity-toity, too good for the rest of us, they've got to be different, haven't they, bloody bohemians the lot of them, load of boozers, junkies, fairies, layabouts, I mean to say, *only nine symphonies, only thirty plays, only ten novels, only ONE Sistine Chapel* (they say he was so pissed he couldn't get up the ladder), I mean, what do you expect?

Et in El Vino ego, Doc. In a small way, of course. What might *I* not have done, be doing, were it not for the lure of the barmaid's pinny and the brass-handled pump? Ah, the first chapters I have! What prolegomena! What flyleaf notes! A thousand words of the best, then it's off to the local for a self-congratulatory belt, and when I roll home, in a day or two, all is ashes, forgotten, dead. How was it going to go on, this trilogy, before those bottles intervened? Who was this character, and this, and who cares, now? Ah, those publishers' lunches, yes, I'll do a novel, yes, I have this wonderful idea, he meets her, see, and they go off to Ensenada, and her husband, broken by drugs and a lifetime of inferior diplomacy, kills his mistress, let's have another bottle of this excellent Mouton Cadet, but their son returns from the Congo where his mercenary activities have involved him with none other than, my goodness this *is* an amicable cognac, oh yes, you should certainly have the first draft by February, as you say, it's a natural, film rights alone should bring us in . . .

And I wake up in a Turkish bath, some time later, and can only remember that I had my umbrella when I left the house, but was it in the cab, or was it in the restaurant, or am I thinking of my raincoat?

Well, that's it, Doc, another thousand words, another bottle. And that's all you'll get from me today. All I ask is that when my liver and I kick off, and the *Journal of Alcoholism* rings up for a few succinct remarks on posterity's loss, you'll recall all this, and understand a little.

It may surprise you, but I'd hate to be remembered as just another greenish-blue liver, shrunk to half its proper size.

Some Day My Prince Will Crawl

"A group of the women's liberation
movement on Merseyside is rewriting fairy
tales, in which men and women will be
shown to have equal opportunities." *The Guardian*

. . . brought it to the home of the two sisters, who did all they
could to squeeze a foot into the slipper. But they could not
manage it.

"Tell me, my good fellow," said the Prince's equerry to their
father, "have you no other daughters?"

"Only Cinderella," he replied.

The two sisters burst out laughing, but the equerry insisted
that she be brought, and when she was brought she sat down,
very shyly, as she was bid; and on putting the slipper to her foot,
the equerry perceived that the latter slid in without trouble,
and was moulded to its shape like wax.

"It is she!" cried the Prince, who could contain himself no
longer. "It is indeed my own true love!" Catching Cinderella's
two hands in his, he murmured softly: "Will you be my Queen?
Will you sit beside me in my great throne-room and . . ."

"*Whose* great throne-room?" snapped Cinderella, who had
begun making a few quick calculations on the equerry's cuff
with a piece of coal. "Either it's *our* great throne-room, baby,
or you find yourself another foot."

The Prince smiled, for he was as good as he was handsome.

"Of course, my own dove," he said softly, "anything you . . ."

"Also," said Cinderella, "I think the kingdom, or rather
queendom, ought to be in my name. Death duties being what
they are, I don't plan to end up taking a bunch of tourists from

Athens, Georgia, round my bathroom at two ducats a time after you snuff it."

"But my sweetest love," said the Prince, "my family has ruled this country since time immem . . ."

Cinderella stubbed her cigarette out on the equerry, and pushing back her green eye-shield, she looked up from her ledger.

"Listen, kid," she said, "either you want a country or a Safari Park And Funfair. You can't have it both ways. This is the fourteenth century. Also, marriage is for the birds: I'm only doing this as a straight business proposition, and if you want a bit of the other, you'll take my advice and stay *shtum*. Now, about my Cabinet reshuffle . . ."

. . . so Little Red Riding Hood took off her cloak, but when she climbed up on the bed she was astonished to see how her grandmother looked in her night-gown.

"Grandmother dear!" she exclaimed, "what big arms you have!"

"All the better to hug you with, my child!"

"Grandmother dear, what big ears you have!"

"All the better to hear you with, my child!"

"Grandmother dear, what big eyes you have!"

"All the better to see you with, my child!"

"Grandmother dear, what big teeth you have!"

"All the better to eat you with, my child!"

With these words, the wicked Wolf leapt upon Little Red Riding Hood, and stopped a short right to the jaw.

"HAI!" cried Little Red Riding Hood, whanging home a textbook karate jab to the ribs that brought the Wolf to its knees.

"AKACHO!" screamed Little Red Riding Hood, following up with a neck chop, a double-finger eye-prod, and a reverse groin kick.

The Wolf coughed, once, and expired on the rug.

At that moment, the door of the little house flew open, and the woodchopper burst in, brandishing his axe.

"Little Red Riding Hood!" he cried, "are you all right?"

"No thanks to you, you fink!" snapped Little Red Riding Hood, snatching the axe from him and, breaking it across her knee, tossing it into the corner. "And while you're at it, wash the dishes!"

With which she cracked her knuckles and strode out into the forest, slamming the door behind her.

. . . and, drawing his broad sword, the Prince hacked his way through the terrible tangle of thorns that had grown up around the palace in the past hundred years. The sight that now met his gaze was enough to fill him with icy fear. The silence of the palace was dreadful, and death seemed all about him. The recumbent figures of men and animals had all the appearance of being lifeless, until he perceived by the pimply noses and ruddy faces of the porters that they merely slept. It was plain, too, from their glasses, in which there were still some dregs of wine, that they had fallen asleep while drinking.

The Prince made his way up the great staircase, where the guards still stood, limp and snoring, and through the rooms of the palace, filled with sleeping lords and ladies, and so came at last to a chamber which was all decked over with gold. There he encountered the most beautiful sight he had ever seen. Reclining upon a bed, the curtains of which were drawn back, was a princess of seemingly some sixteen summers, whose radiant beauty had an almost unearthly lustre.

Trembling in his admiration, he drew near, and bent, and kissed her tenderly upon the sleeping lips. Her eyelids fluttered; her eyes opened; and saw him.

"Don't you ever think about anything else?" she snapped.

. . . and Aladdin found himself alone in the cellar, with only the dirty old lamp and the spiders.

"Mother!" he called, "Mother, I'm down here!"

At that moment, the Widow came into the kitchen and found her wicked brother-in-law standing by the trap-door through which he had just pushed Aladdin.

"Kids!" she shouted. "You give up your best years to them, you slave over them, you bring 'em up, and what do you get?"

"What?" said her brother-in-law.

"Trouble you get!" said the Widow. "Heartaches you get! Are they grateful? Do they know how a mother wears herself out? Believe me, Nat, if I had my time all over again, you know what I'd have?"

"What?" said her brother-in-law.

"A cat I'd have!" said the Widow. "Or a canary, maybe. At least they don't bring a girl home, she's not fit to clean a mother's shoes."

"Mother!" cried Aladdin, "is that you, Mother?"

"When he wants me," said the Widow, "so he calls! God forbid I should want something from him, I have to go down on my bended knees, he should bring the coal in!"

And with that, she kicked the trap-door shut.

"Is that all I'm fit for?" she shouted. "Cooking, slaving, bringing up lousy ungrateful children, they don't have no respect! Is that what being a woman means?" She shrugged, and sighed a heavy sigh. "So tell me, Nat, how's the lamp business?"

"Don't ask," said her brother-in-law.

"What you need," said the Widow, "is a partner. Someone with a shrewd business sense. Someone, she's spent her whole life slaving for nothing, for insults, when she could have been *somebody*, a business brain like hers!"

"It's a small business, Minnie, a turnover, you could fit it in a thimble."

"So we open a second barrow," said the Widow. "A *branch*. So all of a sudden, we're a chain. We knock out present stock as sale goods due to warehouse fire, less than cost, then we go direct to the manufacturers for our new line, cutting out our middle suppliers, and with having multiple outlets we can now place gross orders to take advantage of discount, and after that . . ."

"Minnie," said her brother-in-law, "what a goldmine Sid had in you all these years and he never knew it!"

"From nothing he knew!" said the Widow. "Only from darning and cooking and bringing up kids, what am I, a skivvy, a business head on me like Wossname Rockefeller . . ."

They strolled out into the sunshine together, to inspect the barrow and their immeasurable future. From the cellar, the muffled cries of Aladdin grew fainter, and fainter, and fainter.

GERMANY

The People

Germans are split into two broad categories: those with tall spikes on their hats, and those with briefcases. Up until 1945, the country's history was made by those with spikes. After 1945, it was made by those with briefcases. In common with the rest of Europe, its history is therefore now known as economics. Ethnically, the Germans are Teutonic, but prefer not to talk about it any more. This ethnos was originally triform, being made up of Vandals, Gepidae, and Goths, all of whom emigrated south from Sweden in about 500 BC; why they emigrated is not exactly clear, but many scholars believe it was because they saw the way Sweden was going, i.e. neutral. Physically, Germans are tall and blond, though not as tall and blond as they sometimes think, especially when they are short, dark Austrians with a sense of destiny. When they sing, the Germans link arms and rock sideways; it is best described as horizontal marching.

The Land

The country, or *Lebensraum*, is extremely beautiful and situated in the very centre of Europe, thus lending itself to expansion in any direction, a temptation first succumbed to in the fifth century AD (the *Volkerwanderung*) when Germany embraced most of Spain, and regularly indulged in since. It is interesting to note that this summer there will be three million Germans in Spain, thus outnumbering the first excursion by almost a hundred to one.

The History

For almost two thousand years, Germany was split into separate states that fought one another. In the nineteenth century, they combined and began fighting everyone else.

69

They are currently split up again and once more fighting one another. If they combine, the result is anybody's guess. Having lost the last war, they are currently enjoying a *Wirtschaftswunder*, which can be briefly translated as "The best way to own a Mercedes is to build one." That is about all there is to German history, since no one has ever known what was going on, and if this is the case, then the Truth cannot be said to exist. Germany has, as you can see, provided many of the world's greatest philosophers.

BELGIUM

The People
Belgium is the most densely populated country in Europe, and is at the same time fiercely divided on the subjects of language and religion. This means that it is impossible to move anywhere in the country, which is packed with mobs standing chin to chin and screaming incomprehensible things at one another in the certain knowledge that God is on their side, whoever He is. That there has not been more bloodshed is entirely due to the fact that there isn't room to swing a fist. Consequently, what the Belgian authorities most fear is contraception: if it ever catches on, and the population thins to the point where rifles may be comfortably unslung from shoulders, the entire nation might disappear overnight.

The Land
The land is entirely invisible, except in the small hours of the morning, being for the rest of the time completely underfoot. It is therefore no surprise to learn that Belgium's largest industries are coal and mineral mining, as underground is the only place where there is room to work. Plans have been suggested for reclaiming land from the sea, on the Dutch pattern, but were always shelved as soon as it was realised that there was neither room for the water that would have to

be removed from the sea, nor, alternatively, any spare land to spread to extend the coastline outwards.

The History
Belgium has always suffered horribly at the hands of occupying forces, which, given the overcrowding, is only to be expected. The bayoneting of babies by Prussians, for example, was never intentional; it was simply that it was impossible to walk about with fixed bayonets in such confined spaces without finding something stuck on the end of them. For the same reason, the sprout was developed by Brussels agronomists, this being the largest cabbage a housewife could possibly carry through the teeming streets.

FRANCE

The People
The French are our closest neighbours, and we are therefore bound to them by bonds of jealousy, suspicion, competition, and envy. They haven't brought the shears back, either. They are short, blue-vested people who carry their own onions when cycling abroad, and have a yard which is 3.37 inches longer than other people's. Their vanity does not stop there: they believe themselves to be great lovers, an easy trap to fall into when you're permanently drunk, and the natural heirs to Europe. It has been explained to them that there is a difference between natural heirs and legitimate heirs, but they cannot appreciate subtle distinctions, probably because French has the smallest vocabulary of any language in Europe.

The Land
France is the largest country in Europe, a great boon for drunks, who need room to fall, and consists of an enormous number of bars linked by an intricate system of serpentine cobbles. Exactly why France is so cobbled has never been

fully explained, though most authorities favour the view that the French like to be constantly reminded of the feel of grapes underfoot. The houses are all shuttered to exclude light, as a precaution against hangovers, and filled with large lumpy beds in which the French spend 83.7 per cent of their time recovering from sex or booze or both. The lumpiness is due, of course, to the presence of undeclared income under the mattresses.

The History

French history, or "gloire" starts with Charlemagne, and ends with Charlemagne. Anything subsequent was in the hands of bizarre paranoiacs who thought they were God (Louis XIV) or thought they were Charlemagne (Napoleon) or thought they were God and Louis XIV and Charlemagne and Napoleon (de Gaulle). Like most other European nations, the French have fought everyone, but unlike the rest have always claimed that both victories and defeats came after opposition to overwhelming odds. This is probably because they always saw two of everything.

LUXEMBOURG

The People

There are nine people in Luxembourg, and they are kept pretty busy making stamps. It is not the smallest country in Europe: there are only eight people in Monaco, five in Andorra, and Herr J. F. Klausner in Liechtenstein, so as the fourth non-smallest country in Europe, it enjoys a rather unique position. The people are of middle height, with the small, deft fingers of master-perforators, and all look rather alike, except for their Uncle Maurice who lost an ear on the Somme. They are a rather arrogant people (they refer to World War I as the Battle of Maurice's Ear) but not un-artistic: *My Day At The Zoo*, by the country's infant prodigy, ran into nine copies and won the Prix Maurice for 1969.

The Land

On a clear day, from the terrace of the Salon de Philatelie, you can't see Luxembourg at all. This is because a tree is in the way. Beyond the tree lies Belgium. The centre of the country is, however, very high, mainly because of the chimney on it, and slopes down to a great expanse of water, as they haven't got around to having the bathroom overflow pipe fixed. The climate is temperate (remember that ninety per cent of Luxembourg is indoors) and the local Flora is varied and interesting, especially on her favourite topic, the 1908 five-cent blue triangular.

The History

Old Luxembourg (now the coal-cellar of the modern country), was founded in the twelfth century by King John of Bohemia, who wanted somewhere to keep the lawn-mower. It escaped most of the wars and pestilences that swept Europe in the subsequent eight centuries, often because the people were out when they called, and is therefore one of the most stable political and economic elements in the EEC: its trade-balance is always favourable (imports come in at the back gate and leave by the front door as exports). Luxembourg is also the oldest ally of Stanley Gibbons Ltd., although it is probably most famous as the birthplace of Horace Batchelor.

NETHERLANDS

The People

Like the Germans, the Dutch fall into two quite distinct physical types: the small, corpulent, red-faced Edams, and the thinner, paler, larger Goudas. As one might expect of a race that evolved underwater and subsisted entirely upon cheese, the Dutch are somewhat single-minded, conservative, resilient, and thoughtful. Indeed, the sea informs their entire culture: the bicycle, that ubiquitous Dutch vehicle, was designed to facilitate underwater travel, offering least resistance to waves and weed, the clog was introduced to weigh down the feet and prevent drifting, and the meerschaum pipe, with its characteristic lid, was designed expressly to exclude fish and the larger plankton. And those who would accuse the Dutch of overeating would do well to reflect on the notorious frangibility of dykes: it's no joke being isolated atop a flooded windmill with nothing to eat but passing tulips. You have to get it while you can.

The Land

Strictly speaking, the land does not exist: it is merely dehydrated sea, and concern was originally expressed when the EEC was first mooted that the Six might suddenly turn into the Five after a bad night. Many informed observers believe that this fear is all that lies behind the acceptance of Britain's membership, i.e. we are a sort of First Reserve in case Rain Stops Holland. Nevertheless, it is interesting country, sweeping up from the coastal plain into the central massif, a two-foot high ridge of attractive silt with fabulous views of the sky, and down again to the valleys, inches below. Apart from cheese and tulips, the main product of the country is advocaat, a drink made from lawyers.

The History

Incensed by poor jokes about the Low Countries, the Dutch, having emerged from the sea, became an extremely belligerent people, taking on Spain, France, England, and Austria in quick succession, a characteristic that has almost entirely disappeared from the modern Dutch temperament. It is now found only among expatriate Dutchmen, like Orangemen and Afrikaaners.

ITALY

The People

The median Italian, according to the latest figures of the

Coren Intelligence Unit, is a cowardly baritone who consumes 78.3 kilometres of carbohydrates a month and drives about in a car slightly smaller than he is, looking for a divorce. He is governed by a stable conservative government, called the Mafia, who operate an efficient police force, called the Mafia, which is the official arm of the judiciary, called the Mafia. The Italians are an extremely cultivated folk, and will often walk miles to sell a tourist a copy of the Sistine Chapel ceiling made entirely from sea-shells. They invented the mandoline, a kind of boudoir banjo shaped like a woman's bottom, not surprisingly.

The Land

Italy is boot-shaped, for reasons lost in the mists of geology. The South is essentially agricultural, and administered by local land authorities, called the Mafia; the North is industrial, and run by tightly interlocked corporations, called the Mafia. The largest Italian city is New York, and is linked to the mainland by a highly specialised and efficient communications system, called the Mafia.

The History

Italy was originally called Rome, which came to hold power over Europe by moving into new areas every week or so and threatening to lean on them if they did not fork out tithe (L. *protectio*). It was run by a series of Caesars (Eduardus Gaius Robinsonius, Georgius Raftus, Paulus Munius, etc.) who held sway until the Renaissance, when Leonardo invented the tank and the aeroplane, and thus ushered in modern Italy (in World War II, the Italians, ever brilliant, possessed the only tank with a reverse gear). In the 1920s, the Caesars reasserted themselves in their two main linear branches, the Caponi and the Mussolini, whose symbol was the fasces, which signified "United We Stand," but they didn't.

Farewell My Brownie

"Boy Scouts of the 70s must be prepared
for everything—even to do dirty deeds in
the course of self-defence. An article in the
Warwickshire Scout Group magazine gives
four methods of repelling an attacker who
is employing a bear hug: 1] Thrust two
fingers up his nose. 2] Knee him in the
groin. 3] Scrape a heel down his shin.
4] Stamp on his toes." *Daily Telegraph*

144 West Park Avenue was a dried-out brown house with a
dried-out brown lawn in front of it. There was a beat-up gnome
right in the middle and he was leaning over pretty bad, like
he'd taken on a couple too many last night, and he'd woken up
grey. He was supposed to be holding a fishing-rod, only somebody had snatched it. That can happen, when you hit the
sauce. There's no respect for drunks, these days.

Personally, I was feeling somewhat less good than the gnome
was looking, but I had a job to do. They had this sign in the
window, so I started across. That is, I got to the kerb on my
side of the street. Then this hand is on my arm.

"Excuse me, little boy."

I looked up. There was this old dame and she was giving me
a lot of denture play. I could tell she was after something. She
was pretty big, around five-two, five-three, maybe, and weighing in at about a hundred and twenty. She was carrying an
umbrella with one of those ornate handles. They can be pretty
useful, if you have room to swing them. I went in closer, just
in case. You have to in my business.

"You talking to me, lady?" I said.

"I wondered if you would mind helping me across the road," she said.

I took out a chocolate cigarette and let it hang on my lip for a while.

"Look," I said, and I pointed to my sleeve. "Woodcraft. Semaphore. First Aid. It took a long time to rack up those, lady. I ain't no Wolf Cub."

"I just thought—I mean, the uniform, and—"

I shrugged. It was going to be one of those days. I took her arm. It was wiry, like I expected. I could feel the big Gamages jacknife against my butt. It was heavy. It was good to know it was there.

"Okay, lady, but don't give me no trouble. I wouldn't want to have to kick an old dame in the slats. I just polished the shoes."

We got to the other side, and she hobbled away. She was moving pretty fast. She didn't say thanks. I didn't expect it. All people see is the uniform. Just another lousy Scout. Until they're in trouble. I spat out my cigarette stub. It was getting to taste pretty sour. What can you expect for a shilling a pack? When I hit the big time, I'm going to have nothing but the best cigars. With orange cream right through.

I walked up the path of 144 West Park Avenue, past the gnome. I looked at the sign again. I leaned on the bell. It had one of those chimes, you expect some guy to start reading the nine o'clock news. Then the door opened.

She had class written all over her. And all over her was what I was looking at. She had this cleavage you could walk through without your shoulders touching the material, and her skirt was way above her knees, and she had that sticky red stuff on her mouth that women with class wear and her eyelashes were stuck on pretty good. I see a lot of eyelashes in my business.

"What is it, little boy?" she said.

It was the second time that morning with the little boy routine. Dames seem to like me that way. They're saying it all the time. She had this deep voice I really go for in women. I'm going to have one myself, one of these days. They sound damned good. I gave her a short dry laugh, the kind they dig.

"Is anything wrong?" she said. "Are you lost or something?"

"I just got found," I said. "You have this sign in the window."

"Oh, of course!" she said. "Bob-A-Job. Do you have your card?"

I flashed the scrap at her. It opens a lot of doors. I snapped the wallet shut and stashed it away.

"Let's talk about it inside," I said. I took her arm, and my temperature grabbed a few degrees and started running with them. It was a good arm. My hat kept rubbing her bust. That's the trouble with Scout hats. All rim. But she didn't object. We went into the living-room, and I could tell she didn't pick up her class at the dressmakers. It was an elegant little slum. I expected a maharajah to walk out of the bathroom any minute. They had ducks up the wall and a dog with a lampshade on it and one of them leather calendars from a petrol company. I flipped my hat across the room and it fell in the grate.

"You can't win 'em all," I said. I hit her with the hollow laugh again. We watched the hat smoulder for a bit. She took it out, and poked at it with a long red fingernail.

"It'll be all right," she said. "It's only scorched."

"It ain't the only one," I said. I winked at her for a while.

"Why do you keep blinking?" she said. I could tell she was interested.

"That's winking," I said. "I always do it with both eyes."

"Would you like me to teach you to do it with one?" she said.

"Some other time," I said. "Right now I have a job to do." I opened my top pocket with one hand and took out the pack and shook a couple up to the top and offered it to her.

"Eat?" I said.

She shook her head.

"About the job," I said. "I guess it's the usual story? Your old man is playing around, right? They always do. I'll put a tail on him for a day. When I tail 'em, they stay tailed."

"I don't quite follow."

"It ain't your job. It takes a lifetime. I can recognise forty-six types of tree. And all the ferns there is. If your old man goes into a wood, he ain't going to walk past nothing I don't know about. Also any bus he gets on. I'll know the depot just by looking."

"That's wonderful," she said, kind of funny. I could tell she was pretty tensed up.

"It's what you pay for, baby," I said. "That's all."

"Your cigarette," she said. "It's melting."

I looked down. It had that droop.

"Don't touch the chair," she said. Her voice was high.

"You don't have to tell me about prints, kid," I said. I put on one of these tough grins I have. They like them. "I could tell there was something wrong as soon as I stepped in here. I wouldn't mess things up for the fingerprint boys. Where'd you bury him?"

"I've changed my mind," she said. She stood up.

"That's what they all say. What they forget is, I'm the only friend they got." I took a coin from my pocket and flicked it over, casually. We watched it roll under the sideboard. I shrugged again.

"Easy come," I said, "easy go. If you hit him with an axe, I could get you off with manslaughter. No jury's going to convict a swell-looking—"

"Listen, little boy," she said, "do you want a job or not? I warn you, it's rather dirty?"

I looked at her. I figured my eyes had done a lot for me, so it was about time I returned the favour. So the job was dirty. Was there any other kind? Maybe I should have walked away right then. But I had bills, commitments. There was the *Beano* to buy, and I was getting low on liquorice, and besides, the boys in the Department were relying on me to help chip in for a new bugle. I nodded.

"It's my car," she said. "I'd like it cleaned, inside and out."

So that was it. Her old man had been taken seriously dead right here, and she'd driven the mess off somewhere and dumped it. What she didn't want was signs of the dear departed hanging about on the leather. We went outside. It was a snappy little foreign job, the kind you have the shoe-store measure you for. I figured she would have had to ease the cadaver in with tyre-levers. Dames.

"If you need clean water, just shout."

The legs took her away, and I watched them work for a while. They had a pretty nice job. I wished I could say the same. I opened the door and looked inside. It was pretty filthy. You could have wiped out a cavalry regiment in there and no-one would notice. I was just starting to nose around when I heard these feet rasping on the gravel. I froze.

"Excuse me, young man, but is Mrs. Belwether in?"

I turned around. He was a big guy, forty-ish, but light on his feet. He'd put the Old Spice on with a hose. I let my arms hang loose.

"Who wants her?"

"Prudential Insurance."

I loosed off one of the short dry ones.

"You two don't waste time," I said.

"I'm sorry?"

"I'll just bet. How much was the old guy worth?"

"Look, if I might just have a word with your mummy about her mortgage, I'd be most—"

When I stamped on his toes, the big guy doubled, but he kind of twisted so I couldn't get the fingers up his nose. I got a thumb in his ear, though, and he went down, and he looked sort of surprised, the way they always do. I was moving in on his groin on schedule, when he suddenly got up, and I knew I was in for a fight. He started swinging. I don't know what he was carrying in that briefcase, but it taught me one thing: the insurance business is pretty good these days. It caught me on the side of the cranium, and I went over backwards into the roses, and I fetched up against the gnome. I tried to get at my knife, but it's on one of those spring clips and my dad's the only one who can get it off. I stood up, and I gave him one of my looks instead, but it didn't faze him, and he kept on coming, and he was screaming things. I grabbed my hat and decided to let him take the first round and I set off at a fast canter.

There's a lot of things I'd do for a fast bob, but getting buried ain't one of them.

Red Sky At Night, The Refinery's Alight

Being some extracts from A. Coren's
ENCYCLOPAEDIA OF NEW ENGLISH FOLKLORE

Singing Home the Muck

"Ere she cum, the bubblin scum,
Down from Foskett's Alloys!
Ere cum a dollop o' sunnink brown,
Off of Gribling's Mills!

"There float a poisoned cat,
There go a chokin fish!
Ho hum, tiddle-I-wee,
Here be a sterile newt!

"My ole wife be covered in boils,
My little kid be bald!
Sing Fa-gargle-dong,
All the ducks is dead!"

Just three of the charming verses of *Singing Home The Muck*, a traditional part-song sung by English villagers as, withered arms bare and trousers rolled up to their radioactive knees, they stand at evening in their local water-supply and fish for effluent. Many a night you may come upon them, their heads just visible above the detergent foam, groping for extruded tubes, asbestos waste, rotten fish, crude oil, packing cases, rusty wire, and all the other denizens of stream and rill so highly prized by Englishmen.

Woodworm Tuesday

On Woodworm Tuesday (2nd after Insolvency Sunday, and the first Tuesday of Spring), the traditional Estate Agents' Race is held in villages and hamlets throughout England. Although the origins of this colourful rural event are lost in the mists of chicanery, many anthropologists believe it commemorates the sale in AD 834, after much haggling, of Aelfthrith Cottage, derelict home of the Idiot of Picester, to a merchant of London. As soon as the Idiot took possession of the money and the merchant occupation of the house, the roof, so the story goes, fell in, the doors dropped off, the cesspool overflowed, the foundations sank, and the woodworm, belching the last of the genuine oak beams, immediately "felle upon ye marchaunte and devowred hym hole" (*Chronicle of Mercia*, cap. XVII).

Whatever its folk heritage, the Race itself is a delightfully engaging spectacle: local Estate Agents are required to run the traditional Stonesthrow to the Station, tossing as they run a colour print of a fully modernised thatched cottage standing in two acres of unspoilt woodland, and crying "FIVE HUNDRED POUNDS OR NEAR OFFER! FIVE HUNDRED POUNDS OR NEAR OFFER!" The winner is given as his prize the first media executive of the season to arrive from Knightsbridge, who is directed to the winner's offices by the village Reeve and attendant Virgins of the Parish.

Old Man's Austin

Along England's remoter byways and hedgerows, as the older plants shrivel and disappear, they are rapidly being replaced by colourful clumps of Old Man's Austin, Lady's Mini, Rusty Ford, My Son's Honda, and similar sturdy and enduring growths which, botanists think, may be a natural evolution from such earlier strains as The Common Bedstead, Potty, Grandpa's Mattress, and Sink. Naturally enough, much folk legend has sprung up around the new flora: local people believe, for example, that Broken Windscreen can cause holes in children and that Seeping Oilsump has some weird effect on grass. The Folk Society, in company with the Society for Psychic Research, is also collating a number of reports that, at the time of the full moon, the ghost of Old Pete, the mythical Minister for the Environment, can be seen flitting among the new vegetation, cackling hysterically.

Cublington Fair

A regular event, held in Buckinghamshire, and traditionally associated with Airport Bill, the local name for the Devil. (There are analogues at Stansted and Foulness.)

The Fair begins with a march of Freeholders, usually middle-aged, who parade with quaint hand-lettered signs nailed to long staves which they wave above their heads, shrieking imprecations the while in the hope of averting the curse of Airport Bill, who, they traditionally believe, will appear to them in the form of terrible noises in the sky, and break their greenhouses. After the procession, they gather in a convenient public place and imbibe large quantities of *gin*, traditionally held to be a restorative/aphrodisiac, a clear, aromatic liquid made with money. They then begin to laugh and grope, and vie with one another in creating new oaths directed at their leaders; the evening usually ends when one of these, The Grinning Man, is hanged in effigy.

Fine Afore Seven, Buggies Arter Eleven!

A prophetic shriek, commonest among Southern villagers, though also to be heard in the West Country, Bucks, Berks, and anywhere close to the remains of one of the old Motor Ways, that pattern of dilapidated stone tracks that was laid down by casual primitives in earlier times. The meaning of the phrase is that, if the day's weather has been good, then midnight will see the arrival of the South Kensington Young Boutiquiers' Rally and Bar-B-Q, or similar: these are bands of Little People who come out to play only when England's more beautiful villages are asleep. In their highly coloured vehicles, Mokes and Buggies and Dragsters and the like, decorated with dozens of quartz lights, wind-horns, multi-barrel exhausts, dangle-dollies, borzois, and drunks, they roar through the dark lanes, honking horns, hurling bottles, over-revving, screaming, backfiring, and generally plaguing human beings in a hundred mischievous little ways. Often they kill cats, chickens, dogs, as they go, and, in the morning, their tracks may often be seen on the grass, frequently across gardens, new crops, and village greens. It does not do, so they say, to meddle with them, and most villagers, when the first notes of *Colonel Bogie* trumpet across the moonlit hills, pull the sheets over their heads and try to think of something else.

Up Jack's Pylon

An old game, played by village children, who delight to climb those strange iron constructions which are to be found wherever the countryside is, or was, prettiest, and may be a result of some aberration on the part of Druids. The children scramble to the top of these, and the winner is fused perman-ently to the National Grid.

Blind Ned of Westminster

A persistent figure in English folklore, so much so that there must have been more than one original, as his name crops up throughout the length and breadth of the country. The legend is that at certain times of the year, Blind Ned leaves Westminster and, led by his mad cur, Profit, stalks the land in a bizarre, haphazard fashion, the pattern of which not even the most brilliant students of the arcane have so far been able to divine. And wherever Blind Ned's foot falls, so the legend goes, factories spring up of a loathsome ugliness, and great swathes of mean little boxlike houses, and concrete shopping precincts, and great glass towers; and, hypnotised by the seductive fluting of Blind Ned and the mesmerising dance of Profit, human beings fall in behind them and are borne off to their wretched doom.

Key in The Hat

A time-honoured rite, strongly sexual in undertone, mostly

found in semi-rural areas such as Wates Number 456/32a, Span 447, Happihomes Twelvegrand Plus, and similar instant villages. Lacking more ancient rites to occupy their time, the villagers gather in groups, first at one home, then another, on a strict rota system; and, having absorbed much *gin* (see above) and gone through the ritual Talking—starting with the subject of au pairs, then on to the new Rover, the Permissive Society, louvre doors, Majorca, pot-training, Sainsbury's value, *Elizabeth R*, and the insignificance of pornography (this pattern rarely changes)—they start giggling, and the Host gets his ritual bowler, and all the men throw their car keys into it, and, the partners having been duly selected, everyone goes to bed, where, so the story goes (although there has been little concrete evidence), they talk about au pairs, the new Rover, the Permissive Society, louvre doors, Majorca, pot-training, Sainsbury's value, *Elizabeth R*, and the insignificance of pornography.

If That's The Acropolis, How Come It Don't Chime?

"Robert P. McCulloch imports great
European architecture for reassembly in
new American cities. It was he who got the
idea of buying London Bridge and bringing
it to the planned community of Lake
Havasu City, Arizona. He admits now that
he thought he was buying the more
picturesque Tower Bridge, but adds: 'That
bridge is going to bring in five million
tourists a year'." *Newsweek*

Robert P. McCulloch,
McCulloch Corporation,
Los Angeles, Calif.

5th May

Dear Mr. McCulloch:

Thank you for your wonderful brochure and miraculous unrepeatable offer. Yes, we here at Hogsnout Aerospace Engineering Model Township sure would like to increase our cultural status as mentioned on page 4, and we are over 21. We are a community of forty thousand souls, average family income in excess of $16,000 p.a., and as our town was built during the night of August 10, 1969, we don't have nothing of what you might call hallowed antiquity, always excepting the portrait of my father, Simeon Hogsnout III, painted in 1949 in genuine oils, but this is presently hanging in our boardroom and in consequence not available for our community to enrich its cultural life from. Also, it don't pull in tourists all that good.

Some old European stuff would be just great! My wife and myself went on this $2899 all-inclusive world trip last Fall and we saw a hell of a lot of stuff that would look damn good in the middle of Simeon Hogsnout III Plaza downtown, especially if you have something that would fit in between the Hogsnout Motor Inne and the Simeonburger Parlour and Grill. The area available is about 20,000 sq. ft., with mains drainage and convenient all freeways.

Naturally, I wouldn't want to interfere with no expert authority, but one thing Miriam and me did see was at this Italian place, I guess you'd call it, and they had this old tower, it was leaning over. We went up the top and dropped stuff off like the guide said, on account of they invented gravity up there. This strikes me like a very appropriate cultural thing to have in the middle of the fastest-growing little aerospace industry township in the world!

I know a tower like that would cost approx. $100,000 new, construction industry rates being crazy right now, but this one is extremely secondhand and, like I say, in a very advanced state of lean and God knows about dry rot etcetera, and I reckon I would be doing them a favour taking it off their hands cheap.

I look forward to hearing your esteemed comments.

Yours very truly,
Simeon Hogsnout IV,
President,
Hogsnout Aerospace Inc.

Simeon Hogsnout IV,
Hogsnout Aerospace Inc.

18th May

Dear Mr. Hogsnout:

Thank you for your letter of May 5. I apologise for the delay in replying, but we have been going through our files of old leaning things in an effort to locate the cultural gem of your choice. There is a lot of stuff like you describe in Europe, but

I think what you have in mind is the Leaning Tower of Pisa, and a very wise choice if I might say so, except it will set you back a good five million, if I'm any judge, plus postage and packing. I haven't seen the treasure in question personally, but I guarantee that setting it up in Simeon Hogsnout III Plaza will not only enrich your township but also pull in the hicks, especially if you can get it to lean across the Hogsnout Motor Inne swimming-pool, so's they can maybe dive off it at ten bucks a throw, which has a thick edge over Pisa on account of the cobbles underneath.

I have taken the trouble to enclose a brick of the Leaning Tower, collected by my European sales manager, in the hope it will give you some impression of the quality. A deposit of $50,000 secures.

Yours,
Robert P. McCulloch.

Robert P. McCulloch,
McCulloch Corporation,
Los Angeles, Calif.

24th September

Dear Mr. McCulloch:

Very many thanks for your communication of the 3rd ultimo, also the five truckloads of Leaning Tower of Pisa at $5,000,000, plus ten per cent discount for cash. However, there's one or two things I'd like to enquire about, if you'll excuse me.

I do not pretend to be a leading authority on Europe culture, but we have now unpacked the item and put it up, and it don't seem to be exactly the way I remember it. I could be wrong, but I don't want people should turn up in our community and start being suspicious about our cultural gem, also not shelling out the ten bucks to go up it. Which, as a matter of fact they can't, right now, on account of we got it up all right but when we tried to get it to lean a little, it kind of broke. And when it broke, the top fell off, and when we took a close look at it, this turned out to be a cement guy with one arm and one eye and a

89

triangular hat. Miriam says she don't remember no guy on the top.

Yours truly,
Simeon Hogsnout IV.

Simeon Hogsnout IV,
Hogsnout Aerospace Inc.

3rd October

Dear Mr. Hogsnout:

Like I told you originally, I have not inspected this Leaning Tower personally, but I was always under the impression that it had a guy on the top, plus four lions underneath which you will notice I threw in free, gratis and for nothing. As these lions alone would normally run out at a minimum of ten grand apiece, I do not understand all the beefing on your part. It is my opinion that the cement guy is Sir Isaac Garibaldi, who invented gravity, like you say. It may be that when you and your lady wife was up the tower on your original trip, you was standing underneath the statue and didn't notice it. No doubt when you finally get the thing in one piece and leaning like it's supposed to, you will recognise it. It's no good looking at a cultural treasure like this in bits, unless it's the Eiffel Coliseum, or something, which is way outside your price range, anyhow.

Yours,
Robert P. McCulloch.

Robert P. McCulloch,
McCulloch Corporation,
Los Angeles, Calif.

9th October

Dear Mr. McCulloch:

Never mind the cracks about my price range, I already had to pay out another fifty thousand bills to repair this thing which is beginning to cause adverse comment in our community, particularly from Jack Hammell, our foremost used car dealer and a person of some standing, who has been to Europe in both wars and reckons that what I have bought is the British Great Fire Monument, only the big brass ball is missing from the top, rendering it worthless in Jack's opinion, and mine, too, if you want to know. What we appear to have is the cheap part of a Leaning Great Fire Monument, and there ain't nobody going to pay good money to see that, especially as the only way we can get it to lean and stay up is by propping it against the Hogsnout Motor Inne, which has now been condemned as unfit for human habitation on account of it's got this giant thing leaning on it.

However, I do not wish to appear a sore loser. If you will agree to remove this item and replace it with something similar in a nice lightweight plastic, I am prepared to consider the matter closed.

Yours truly,
Simeon Hogsnout IV.

The Culture Slaves

"Why," I cried, beating my fist happily upon the topaz-glass surface of our unimaginably *au courant* breakfast-table (Zarach and David Hicks, 110 Fulham Road, only £298) with such force that the Matabele carved soapstone box which holds our family Sweetex fell over and woke our lemming, "this kedgeree is superb!"

My wife, ravishing in her fashionable Vietnam battle fatigues, turned the bacon deftly with her bayonet and blushed.

"Thank you, dearest," she murmured, an early Victorian epithet gaining much currency in our circle, "it is, in fact, a recipe for ferret stew from the *Che Guevara Book of Guerilla Cooking, as told to Clement Freud*. I had to queue all night to get my copy from Now Books (Hampstead). It was just like the war."

"How super!" I cried, hoping the word had survived the night.

"Yes. Vanessa was in front of me, and Antonia was right behind, and we kept awake by establishing a dialogue on East Pakistan with passing workers."

"Wonderful!" I said, filleting a paw. "Any reaction?"

"They told us to eff off," she said. "It was so stimulating."

"Only connect," I murmured. "The gut reaction is all."

We paused to allow our two-year-old, who had just come in to the kitchen, to pee in the dishwasher. A shiver of gratitude ran through us at his irrepressiblity, and our eyes met. We would have made love there and then, to continue the mood of freedom he had initiated, but he might have thought it self-conscious, so we desisted. He is instantly suspicious of deliberate attempts at non-verbal communication, and tends to strike out with his hammer whenever he senses condescension.

"Would you like to go to Galt Toys this morning, Giles?" I asked him.

"Giles kill cat," he said, and went out onto the patio to look for suitable rocks.

"Galt's have an exhibition of Rumanian toys today," I explained to my wife. "They are mainly large unpainted wooden blocks, approved by psychologists throughout the Warsaw Pact countries, and only a fiver apiece. The child may call them 'train' or 'horse' or 'womb' as the mood takes him. As an experiment in pre-pubescent object-dissociation, it could hardly be bettered."

She speared a sizzling rasher and landed it, and sat down beside me on her chromium tractor-seat. The Calder mobile hanging above the stove paused, struck by a last spurt of flying fat, and began to revolve slowly in the opposite direction.

"I don't see how we could fit it in," she said, carefully.

I removed a rib from my teeth.

"But surely," I said, "we are free between 11 a.m. and 11.40?"

She hesitated, and the rasher trembled between her chopsticks.

"I don't know how to tell you this," she said, "but I'm afraid that the only tickets I could get for the Chitrasena Dance Company of Ceylon are for this afternoon's matinee."

"*What!*"

"I knew you'd be upset," she murmured.

"But can't you see what this means?" I shouted, with such force that our mynah bird woke up and began quoting Henry James in a beaky undertone. "If we have to visit them this afternoon, then we shall have to bring forward our visit to the W. H. Patterson Gallery to this morning, if we don't want to miss The Works of The Family Koekkoek, which means we shall have no time to see the Intercraft exhibition of Danish System Furniture until *after* the bloody dancers, so that we shan't be able to catch Buster Keaton at Academy One, thereby robbing ourselves of the chance to see *Three Ages* for the fourth time, which is one more than George Weidenfeld."

"I know," she whispered, "I know."

"Similarly, as one might, given a condition whereby expediency, so to speak, would not take priority over, if you like, probity, or alternatively," cackled the mynah bird, "some form of ingestive process, by which we might, so we desired, take . . ."

"And if," I shrieked, hurling a Minoan fragment at the bird, "we are forced to see Keaton at the evening performance, then we shall not be present at the first night of *Bum* at the Round House . . ."

". . . and if we therefore see *Bum* tomorrow night, then we can't possibly get down to Chichester for . . ."

". . . *Caesar and Cleopatra*, which means that we'll have to go the following night and put off *Hobson's Choice* at Pitlochry until Friday, thereby . . ."

". . . missing Friday's Late Night Film on BBC 1, which happens to be . . ."

". . . don't remind me! I can't stand . . ."

". . . HUMPHREY BOGART IN *CASABLANCA!*"

I fell back, broken. Outside, a cat spat. Behind me, the mynah, furious, began reciting *Washington Square*, backwards. Wearily, I reached for my abacus, my graph paper, my Ordnance Survey Map, my *Good Food Guide* and my *Time Out*, and began to calculate. After half an hour (during which time my wife managed to master the last few Regency hallmarks that had up until then eluded her), I threw down my fibre pen in triumph.

"Right!" I cried. "All is rearranged: though it means we shall have to leave next Thursday week's performance of the Moscow State Circus half-way through the juggling bears, and miss the drag tribute to the Dolly Sisters at the Duke of Fife next Friday altogether, I believe we may still save some shred of cultural self-esteem! But hurry, we have not a moment to lose!"

Pausing only to stuff a few clothes into a suitcase and slip our child into bed beside our two inseparable au pair boys, we hurled ourselves into the street. It was a-teem with clunking cars, bouncing like dodgems as our neighbours, grey-faced and raspberry-eyed, jockeyed for position as they set course for

the Open Space, and Whitechapel Art Gallery, and the Malt-
ings, and Edinburgh, and the Hayward, and Glyndebourne,
and Camden Passage, and Gimpel Fils, and the Purcell Room,
and the Paris-Pullman, and the Queen Elizabeth Hall, and
Glastonbury, and the ICA, and Stratford, and anywhere else
where people of ton, taste and kultur may be found.

As we sprang to the only unoccupied cab, a dark hirsute
figure leapt between us and grabbed the door-handle, scatter-
ing snuff and polysyllables.

"Brian!" I cried, for it was indeed noted columnist and wit
Brian Allen, bound, no doubt, for some tryst of pith and value.
He turned, wild-eyed, and beat at me dementedly with his
tweed hat.

"Gerroff!" he shrieked. "I am already late for the private
view of Felicien Rops engravings, on which I have commis-
sioned myself to write at least twelve articles, and unless I can
see it in time to make my connection for Paddington and this
afternoon's Death Of Acteon Charity Walk From Worthing To
Littlehampton, I shall not be home in time for *Magic Rounda-
bout!*"

I ducked his hat, and jabbed him with my *Penguin Albinoni
Scores;* falling, he grasped my sleeve in a final effort, but his
hand, enfeebled through typing, merely plucked and dropped.
We left him there, and leapt aboard.

Euston was alive with citizens of taste, rushing hither and
yon from guichet to guichet in a desperate attempt to match
festivals to timetables. As I ran towards the grille for Glasgow
and Pitlochry, I was almost bowled over by a small blond
publisher.

"My dear Tony!" I exclaimed. "Off to Pitlochry, too?"

Swiftly, he concealed a burgeoning sneer behind his friend's
hand.

"I've *done* Pitlochry, choochie," he said, "hasn't everyone?
We're going down to Bournemouth to catch the try-out of the
new Harold. Isn't everybody?"

I reeled, stricken.

"I didn't realise!" I cried. "Nobody told me!" I fumbled for my notepad. "Quick, what's it called, I'll try to catch it on Thur—"

"Sorry, love, must fly," he shouted, already breaking into a trot, "if I miss it today, I'll have to see it in London, and if word were to get around that I actually wait until things come to *London*, I might as well be seen eating Maltesers at *The Sound Of Music!*"

He was gone, mincing to glory and new horizons. Chastened, we took our seats in our compartment and tried to catch up on a little reading, but the encounter had shaken me and I found my attention unaccountably wandering from *Bayerische Wortspiele des XVIIten Jahrhunderts*. My wife, noticing my sighs, glanced up from her portable potter's wheel.

"Is anything wrong?" she said.

I watched her nascent urn decelerate and wilt.

"Oh, nothing, just—well—how in God's name can we ever know if we've made the right decision! Should we have plumped for Pitlochry on the day the Royal National Eisteddfod opened at Bangor? Are we perhaps narrowing our cultural sights too much? Should we not have gone instead to the Pig Fair at Ballycastle, Co. Antrim, and wrestled for a prize ham? Or cheered on the Traction Engine Rally at Widmerpool? There is too much to see! There is too much to experience! How can we ever know that we have made the right cultural decision? Remember when the Bookbang was on and we missed *The Three Stooges Go To Mars* at the Bioscope, Uxbridge?"

"And everyone who was anyone saw it twice."

"Quite! Remember when we deliberately refused to go to see Nat Jackley as Buttons at the Winter Gardens, Blackpool, because we were sure pantomime was old hat, and we went to a Happening at the Open Space instead?"

"Only nothing Happened, because everyone was . . ."

". . . in Blackpool." I bit my knuckle, while timetables and reviews and programme notes and words-of-mouth jangled in my head. "How can we *know?*" I cried.

The train slowed for Bletchley, and I sprang to my feet, hauling down our bags.

"I have gone cold on Pitlochry!" I cried. "We shall instead turn back to London and attend the Osborne party for *Times* Letters To The Editor co-signatories. I have not supported pot, *Oz*, Bangla Desh, the gaslights on Constitution Hill, the EEC, Soviet Jewry, the British Museum, Foulness, and the first cuckoo for nothing! In my opinion, Cheyne Walk is where tonight's most significant cultural thing is happening!"

Relieved, we touched the platform before the train had stopped. But we were not alone: among those baling out of the carriages were some of the noblest stockbrokers, publishers, journalists, financiers, and culture-formers in the country. Our hearts, warmed at the brotherhood, leapt!

"To the Osbornes, then!" I cried, as we sped for the down platform.

"To the Mime Workshop, Canonbury!" screamed a voice in the mob.

We eyed one another feverishly, on the run.

"To the Young Vic!" howled another, and "To the Everyman, Hampstead!" a third, while, behind us, two portly men, hands linked, set up a breathless chant: "To *Pork!* To *Pork!*"

Our pace slackened. We all stopped. Our eyes searched back and forth and met only other searching eyes. Beyond the station, the flat Bucks lands stretched far and darkling.

We were in the middle of nowhere.

**According to a new publishing company,
Enfance Publishing, "every leading author
has at least one children's book in him."**
Every **leading author?**

From THE GOLLIES KARAMAZOV
by Fyodor Dostoyevsky

On a bitterly cold morning towards the end of November, 18—
a pale young man left his little room at the top of a toadstool in
one of the meaner tree-roots of the province of Toyland, and
began to descend the dark and freezing stairs.

He was praying that he would not meet his landlady. Her
burrow gave directly onto the corridor, and he had to pass it
every time he went in or out. The door was usually open, and
he would have to run past to avoid seeing Mrs. Rabbitoyeva,
and when he did so he would experience a sensation of terror
which left him shaking and sick to his stomach. Sometimes he
would be physically sick. Other times, he would become possessed of a hacking and terrible cough, and his thin little body
would grow luminous with sweat.

It was not merely that he was behind with his rent, living as
he did in wretched poverty: it was simply that he had of late a
horrible fear of meeting anybody, of engaging them in the
lightest of conversations, of remarking upon the weather. This
fear had itself become a sickness. Mrs. Rabbitoyeva, if she saw
him, would wipe her paws on her apron (an action which itself
brought an uncontrollable trembling to the young man's
emaciated limbs, and set the pattern on his threadbare herring-

bone overcoat twitching like a nest of spiders), and smile, and nod, and say:

"Good morning, Noddy Noddeyovich! I have a nice worm ragout cooking on the stove for your lunch."

Or:

"You should have a young lady, Noddy Noddeyovich! It is not right for a fine young man to spend so much time in the company of gnomes."

At this, the young man would fall to the ground and kiss the hem of her garment.

But on this occasion, Mrs. Rabbitoyeva called Noddy Noddeyovich into her kitchen, and, despite the fearful trembling of his limbs which set the bell upon his cap tinkling like some derisory omen of imminent doom, he followed her. He counted his steps, as he always did—eleven, twelve, thirteen, to the table, fourteen, fifteen, to the workbench, where the knives were, and the big meat chopper. The kitchen smelt of boiled sedge, and old ferret offal, and the grey, fatty soup that Mrs. Rabbitoyeva always kept simmering for the pitiful little civil servants who inhabited her dark, cold building.

"Noddy Noddeyovich," said Mrs. Rabbitoyeva, "I wish to talk with you about the Gollies Karamazov."

His trembling worsened. The Gollies Karamazov had recently moved in to the room next to Noddy Noddeyovich, and they came from the Big Wood, and their faces were black as round holes in the white winter ice. Whenever Noddy Noddeyovich saw them, he began to shake all over, and often he was sick down the stairwell, and sometimes he fainted altogether. He did not want to talk about the Gollies Karamazov. He listened for a while to the sound of Mrs. Rabbitoyeva, and it was of no sense, a heavy buzz, like the flies upon the far steppes when spring wakes the eggs.

And then he picked up the big meat chopper, and he brought it down on Mrs. Rabbitoyeva's old head, and she looked very surprised, and when the blood was all over his hands, their trembling stopped.

"I should not be here," said Noddy Noddeyovich, possibly

aloud. "Soon Plod Plodnikov of the State Police will be here for his morning glass of tea, and he may engage me in some philosophical discussion about guilt, with reference to the words of Morotny, and it would be better if I were to get in my little car and go Beep! Beep! and seek the advice of Bigears Bigearsnitkin . . ."

From FIVE GO OFF TO ELSINORE
by William Shakespeare

ACT ONE, Scene 1
Cheam, a desert country near the sea. Before the gates of The Laburnums.
Alarums off. Sennets. Keatons. Enter Julian.

Julian: Hung be the heavens with black, yield day to
          night!
          The hols are but a short week old, and now
          There comes such news as Hecate herself
          Would quake to hear of! Five years of study
            gone
          And now I learn that all I have to show
          Is two O-levels: one Eng. Lit., one Maths!
          Five subjects failed, and I one subject felled
          By failure to as fell a fall as folly
          Feels!

Enter Timmy, a dog.

                  Ah, Timmy! Had I but the joy
          Of e'en thy meanest flea, I were in luck!

Timmy: Arf! Arf!

Julian: Unmetric!

Timmy: Arf! Arf! Arf! Arf! Arf!

Julian (*weeps*): The very dogs do bend them to my pleas,
          Though men do reck me not! But yet I'm
            wrecked!

Enter Georgina.

Georgina: How now, sweet coz! I am this sec arrived
          From Cheltenham Ladies' College for the vac!

	And we shall do such things, we Famous Five—

And we shall do such things, we Famous Five—
Find maps, thwart thieves, have midnight feasts
In ruined castles, smugglers' coves, and more
Deserted cottages than you've had hot—

Julian: Eff off, Georgina! All has come to nought!
A sound career with ICI is lost!
And I must hie me with my measly two
And seek emolument as Clerk (Grade IV).
No longer mine, the tree-house and the barge,
The secret passage and—but ho! What comes?

Enter Dick and Anne.

Dick: Look, dearest Anne! We Five are now conjoined
As one, like some great Lyons Sponge Cake late
Divided, and now once more new enseamed!

Julian (*aside*): It is my younger brother. Dare I ask
How he has fared in this last GCE?
Holloa, sweet Dick! How goes the world
   withal?

Dick: Withal, indeed! With all six subjects passed,
Geog., Maths, Eng. Lit., French, History, and
   Stinks!

Anne: Oh, rippin', Dick! Top-hole, spot on, good
   show!

Julian (*aside*): This little twit shall yet undo me quite!
Replace me in our father's rheumy sight,
And get a Morris Minor for his pains,
The dirty swot! I say, chaps, what about
A game of harry cricket?

All: YES!

Timmy: Arf! Arf!

Enter cricket bag. Stumps are set up. Julian bowls the first ball to Dick, who smites it mightily.

Anne: See Timmy run! Run, Timmy, run! Oh, look!
He's caught the ball between his teeth. Good dog!

Timmy: Arf! Arf! (*Dies*)

Dick: That ball! 'Tis poisoned! It was meant for me!
But what about this bat?

101

Julian:	'Tis poisoned, too!
Dick:	Then have at thee, foul villain! Take thou that!
Julian:	A poisoned off-drive! I am slain, alas! (*Dies*)
Dick:	And so am I! Oh what a measly show! (*Dies*)

Flourish. Enter bearers. They bear the bodies and exeunt.

Georgina (*weeps*): Oh, world! The curse of thy eleven-plus!
Two brothers minus! Shall it aye be thus?

From THE POOH ALSO RISES
by Ernest Hemingway

It snowed hard that winter. It was the winter they all went up to the Front. You could get up early in the morning, if you were not wounded and forced to lie in your bed and look at the ceiling and wonder about the thing with the women, and you could see them going up to the Front, in the snow. When they walked in the snow, they left tracks, and after they had gone the snow would come down again and pretty soon the tracks would not be there any more. That is the way it is with snow.

Pooh did not go up to the Front that winter. Nor did he lie in bed and look at the ceiling, although last winter he had lain in bed and looked up at the ceiling, because that was the winter he had gone up to the Front and got his wound. It had snowed that winter, too.

This winter he could walk around. It was one of those wounds that left you able to walk around. It was one of those wounds that did not leave you much more.

Pooh got up and he went out into the snow and he went to see Piglet. Piglet had been one of the great ones, once. Piglet had been one of the *poujadas*, one of the *endarillos*, one of the *nogales*. He had been one of the greatest *nogales* there had ever been, but he was not one of the greatest *nogales* any more. He did not go up to the Front, either.

Piglet was sitting at his usual table, looking at an empty glass of *enjarda*.

"I thought you were out," said Pooh.

"No," said Piglet. "I was not out."

"You were thinking about the wound?" said Pooh.

"No," said Piglet. "I was not thinking about the wound. I do not think about the wound very much, any more."

They watched them going up to the Front, in the snow.

"We could go and see Eeyore," said Pooh.

"Yes," said Piglet. "We could go and see Eeyore."

They went out into the snow.

"Do you hear the guns?" said Pooh.

"Yes," said Piglet. "I hear the guns."

When they got to Eeyore's house, he was looking at an empty glass of *ortega*. They used to make *ortega* by taking the new *orreros* out of the ground very early in the morning, before the dew had dried, and crushing them between the *mantemagni*, but they did not make it that way any more. Not since the fighting up at the Front.

"Do you hear the guns?" said Eeyore.

"Yes," said Pooh. "I hear the guns."

"It is still snowing," said Piglet.

"Yes," said Eeyore. "That is the way it is."

"That is the way it is," said Pooh.

Believe Me

"My wife says I could do anything I set my
mind to. She says Lew, you could be Pope
if you wanted to". *Sir Lew Grade, in the Sunday Times*

As the papal secretary breathed the heavy doors open and tip-
toed me into the lush executive cell of the Vatican penthouse
suite, the Pope backed, waving, off the balcony, and turned.
He flicked his Romeo y Julieta into a convenient paten, and
glanced at me, a shade uncertainly.

"So who's this?" he said.

"It's your audience for ten a.m., Your Holiness," murmured
the secretary.

"One man?" said the Pope. "You call that an audience?"

"I shan't be very long, Your Holiness," I said, dropping my
eyes respectfully. "I realise it's a busy time."

"Ten o'clock Sunday morning, he realises it's a busy time,"
said the Pope to his secretary. He looked at me over a new cigar.
"It's a peak period, dolly," he said, between sucks. "*The* peak
period, maybe. We got five hundred million people tuned in,
world wide. What do you think the Episcopalians have got?"

"I've no idea, Your Holiness."

"Last week they had nine million. Top whack. The Metho-
dists, five, maybe six million. It's all happening on this channel,
dolly. You know why?" he leaned forward across the desk and
charts. "Because here we give the people what they want!
We give them *colour*. Pageantry. Right, Cyril?"

"Right, Your Holiness," said a pale man in scarlet.

"You know Monsignor Bennett, I take it?" said the Pope.
I shook my head. "Best theologian I got. Talented. Loyal.

104

And not even related. It's what we always say, isn't it Cyril, give the people a good costume drama, you'll run forever. That's what they want at the weekend, dolly. You spend the week sweating your guts out in some dreary office, you schlep backwards and forwards on the lousy train, comes the weekend who wants to sit in some Baptist chapel, they don't even have a stained glass window? No incense, no robes, no nothing. You got a priest, he's wearing a three-piece suit, you call that a *show?*" He indicated the Papal Guard, immobile by the walls of his office, the sunlight winking off their cuirasses, their doublets slashed with tangerine and violet. ' *That's* what I call a show! My schwarzers."

"I think you mean switzers, don't you, Your Holiness?"

There was a long silence while he looked at me. The blue smoke floated between us, dangerously calm.

"A thinker we got here, Cyril," he said at last. "An intellectual. What are you, son, some kind of Jesuit?"

"Oh no, Your Holiness," I said.

"So long as I know," said the Pope. "All I'm short of is Jesuits, they're coming in and out all day nagging about falling standards, nagging about how we ought to have a second channel, nagging about how it used to be intellectual and how the Church is going to the dogs." He sighed, heavily. "I got two hundred million looking in from South America, they haven't got bread to eat, what do they want to know from intellectual content? Give 'em a statue, once a year it has a good cry, that's what pulls 'em in. What's wrong with sentimentality, that's what I want to know? If I listened to the Jesuits, every Sunday we'd get sermons on Aramaic bleeding cruces. After six months of that, we'd have audience figures that'd make *Late Night Line-Up* look like *The Golden Shot*. We'd have two hundred million Anglicans in South America, right, Cyril?"

"Right," said Monsignor Bennett. "Which is why we've put these new saints under contract."

"Which is why we've put these new saints under contract," said the Pope, nodding. He looked up at me, anticipating the query. "We got too many downbeat saints in the Church altogether," he said. "Who wants to know from people, they get on well with animals, or they're shot full of arrows, there's blood everywhere? Where's the entertainment in people burning at the stake or getting ate by lions? Or someone, they took his liver out and left it in the sun? You call that family entertainment?"

"You're getting rid of some of the traditional saints?" I asked.

"Getting rid I don't like," said the Pope. "We're writing some of the draggier ones out of the script, is all. If the public writes in, who knows, maybe we'll bring 'em back in the autumn. Right now we're working on some new ones, topical, moving—we got this one, the fella is an aristocrat, good-looking, all this money he doesn't need to lift a finger, and they're on this million-pound yacht off Bermuda it's full with these beautiful birds, all of a sudden it starts sinking, so what does he do, he goes down in the basement of this boat and he sticks his finger in the hole so's everyone can get off, and when they're off he takes his finger out to follow them, and naturally it goes down like a stone."

"And him with it," said Monsignor Bennett, catching a sob.

"And him with it," said the Pope. "We got Roger Moore posing for the commemorative windows already."

"But he's still alive," I said.

"In Ecuador they know Roger Moore's alive?" said the Pope. "Do me a favour! Anyway, this saint just *looks* like Roger. Like the one who only looks like Tony."

"Curtis?"

"Who else? He's very big right now. He's worth, who knows, maybe fifty million new converts."

"Sixty million," said Cyril.

"Sixty million," said the Pope. "This hi-jacker, this Communist, he's just pulled a gun on this airliner it's got all the Miss World contestants on it, when all of a sudden our martyr gets up and grabs the gun. Unfortunately he gets a coupla holes in the kishkes, but he dies in the arms of Miss Guyana! What a way to go, eh, Cyril?"

"Please God by me," said Monsignor Bennett, crossing himself.

"We're building him his own cathedral out of petty cash," said the Pope. "It's a big promotion. Every October 10, we all get the day off on account of him."

"Tell him about the comic saint," said the Monsignor.

"Nearly forgot," said the Pope. "It's Cardinal Delfont's idea. This fella dies laughing, see? Someone like Marty Feldman, maybe, or Tommy Cooper. Very up-beat. Very nice for the kids." The Pope grabbed a phone suddenly, and dialled. "Monty? Lew. Look, suppose he falls down this flight of stairs? That's right, a touch of your Norman Wisdoms. Who *cares* about expense, Monty? This could be very big."

He banged the phone down impatiently.

"Cardinal Berman," he explained. "All he thinks about is geld. He wants to do it with puppets, if you don't mind!"

"Puppets?"

"Like *Thunderbirds*. His trouble is, he's living in the past. He says puppets is cheaper than Norman Wisdom. All I'm short of, a canonised puppet! Maybe he'd like Sooty!" He snatched the phone again. "MAYBE YOU'D LIKE SOOTY!" he shouted.

"Don't upset yourself, Your Holiness," said Monsignor Bennett. "Tell the kid about the oldies."

"Oldies But Goldies," emphasised the Pope. "There's been a big falling-off at midnight masses," he said. "People don't want to stay up late for a load of old rubbish, right? So we're doing some re-runs of old miracles?"

"Old miracles?" I said.

"They're the best," said the Pope. "Everybody likes to see 'em again. Remember The Raising Of Lazarus?"

"And The Loaves And Fishes," said Monsignor Bennett. "I missed that first time around."

The Pope looked at him irritatedly.

"Who didn't?" he snapped. "That's my whole point, dolly.

We run a series of late-nite miracles in every church in the world. We'll pack 'em in. 'Course," he continued, "we may have to cut them a bit."

"Here and there," said Monsignor Bennett. "People won't notice."

"It could go over very big in the States," said the Pope. "Like our new confessional."

"I'm sorry?" I said.

"You go in this soundproof box, you put on the earphones, and you try for sixty-four aves and a chance to go on the Excommunication Trail."

"The Excommunication Trail?" I exclaimed.

"I know what you're thinking," said the Pope, "and you're right. But it's just a question of ironing the bugs out, that's all. In my opinion, it's a natural."

"A natural," said the Monsignor.

I closed my notebook.

"It all sounds terribly, terribly exciting," I said. "And I'm sure it'll send figures soaring. There's one thing, of course, that would do more to establish you in the ratings than anything else, I mean, it could pull in untold millions of people, it could—"

"Is he talking about some new kind of programme?" asked Monsignor Bennett, disturbed. "Something we haven't thought of?"

"I know what he's talking about," said the Pope. He looked at me penetratingly. "Didn't I say he was smart? Didn't I say he had a head on his shoulders? He's talking about a Second Coming, aren't you, son?"

I nodded, shyly.

"It could send you right to the top," I said. "Are you doing anything about it?"

"Is it in my hands?" said the Pope, spreading them. "So tell me, what is there to do?"

"You could always pray," I said.

The Pope looked up at Monsignor Bennett.

"These modern kids," he said despairingly, "what do they know?"

Once I Put It Down, I Could Not Pick It Up Again

A couple of years ago, some organisation calling itself the Encyclopaedia Britannica sent me twenty-three books to review. Like any reviewer faced with such a task, I wasn't able, of course, to read any of them — just snatched a quick look at the titles on the spines and made a few shrewd guesses.

A. ANSTEY

F. Anstey, author of *Vice-Versa*, *The Brass Bottle*, and many other best-sellers, was one of the most famous figures in Victorian London. A. Anstey wasn't. This, indeed, was the nub of his personal disaster, a searing comment on nineteenth-century society, told for the first time in this splendid volume. A. Anstey was constantly being introduced at smart Victorian soirées to people whose instant reaction was "Not *the* Anstey?" to which he would immediately answer "No, just *a* Anstey, ha-ha-ha!" This pitiful little quip commended him to no-one, and was usually met with a sneering "You mean *an* Anstey" and a snub. He endured this for eighteen years before finally hanging himself in a rented room just off Lewisham High Street.

ANT BALFE

When General Tom Thumb crowned a successful fairground tour with a command performance in front of Queen Victoria, the seal was set on a midget-vogue of staggering proportions. Country fairs and London theatres alike were filled with talented dwarfs, each tinier than the last. The smallest and indubitably the most adroit of these (he could play

Mozart's four horn concertos on a drinking-straw while riding on a stoat) was Ant Balfe, so called because of his incredible diminutiveness. Who knows to what figurative heights he might not have risen, had he not, at his Drury Lane premiere, been trodden on by an inept autograph-hunter?

BALFOUR BOTH

A fascinating tale of Georgian surgery, this recounts the earliest known sex-change operation, on the unfortunate Geraldine (née Gerald) Balfour. It seemed successful at first, and the happy Geraldine took to signing herself G. Balfour (Miss), but subsequent developments proved this course to be premature, and soon she was sending letters of complaint to the General Medical Council signed G. Balfour (Both). Eventually, the name was changed by deed poll to Balfour-Both to avoid upsetting pre-permissive sensibilities. Beautifully illustrated.

BOTHA CARTHAGE

An exceptionally well-documented life of Hannibal, whose dying words give the book its intriguing title. His actual words, apparently, were "Bugga Carthage!" but the publishers, I understand, felt that this might have meant rejection by W. H. Smith, and compromised accordingly.

CARTHUSIANS COCKCROFT

Subtitled "An Edwardian Tragedy", this bitter book tells the story of Thomas Cockcroft, perhaps the most promising Senior Master in Charterhouse's history. He was due for appointment to the headmastership at the incredibly early age of thirty, when certain facts were made public by a disgruntled porter concerning the intimate teas to which Cockcroft would invite the smaller boys. Inevitably, the yellow press dubbed him Carthusians Cockcroft at his infamous trial (*The Daily Graphic* even tried to christen him Fag Cockcroft, but the multi-entendres were too much for its working-class readership), and upon his release from Brixton, he went off to the Congo to shoot porters. There is a statue of him in Chisholm St. Mary, erected in error.

COCKER DAIS

Perhaps the best loved of the East End flyweights, Cocker Dais at one time held the British, British Empire, and European titles. At the peak of his career, he fought an unknown American for the World title, and was knocked out in the second minute of the first round. His pub, *The Cocker Dais*, later became a famous dockside landmark for German bombers.

DAISY EDUCATIONAL

A poignant, heart-warming novel about an elderly schoolmistress in a tiny Welsh village. The influence of *How Green Was My Valley* is, of course, observable, but the presence of a black Druid boutique owner gives the book an essentially modern air.

EDWARD EXTRACT

I'm delighted that the publishers have seen fit to reprint this little-known eighteenth-century novel by Tobias Sterne, because it's a narrative gem of the first water. A bawdy, picaresque romp, it tells how postboy Edward Extract makes off with Squire Weasel's buxom daughter Phyllis, loses her to a Turkish mercenary during the Battle of Blenheim, makes his way to Utrecht disguised as an alternative Pope, falls in love with Warty Eva of Bosnia, is press-ganged into the Hungarian navy, loses his leg at Malplaquet, seduces a lady-in-waiting to Queen Anne, becomes a Whig, loses his right arm at Sheriffmuir, gets Gräfin von Immel with child, goes deaf during the siege of Belgrade, abducts a Moorish slave-girl, and returns at last to his native Suffolk, where he knocks out his left eye on a broken wainshaft. Lusty, purgative, rollicking, and highly recommended.

EXTRADITION GARRICK

It is said that when Lord Chief Justice Sir Esmond Garrick (1789-1852) was refused his request to the Brazilian authorities to extradite Bloody Ned Magee on a charge of treason, he sailed personally to Sao Paulo, strode into the Court of Justice, decapitated the President of the Brazilian Supreme Court, and, turning to the other judges and waving his bloody sabre above his wig, cried: "I would remind ye that English law is based on precedent, and I have just created one!" Magee was released forthwith, and duly hanged at the notorious Vile Assize of 1828. As Extradition Garrick, Sir Esmond pursued an inflexible hunt for refugee criminals, often giving up his holidays to root about in the stews of Marseilles and Cadiz, heavily disguised, in his inexorable search for what he called "hanging fodder", frequently bringing them back to England in a gunny-sack. A thundering good read.

GARRISON HALIBUT

I was bored by this long, scholarly thesis on the Minneapolis dry-goods salesman who rose to be the Governor of Minnesota and is chiefly remembered as the initiator of off-street parking.

HALICAR IMPALA

If you like books that take the lid off the motor industry, then this is for you! Spurred on by what they thought was going to be the enormous success of the Ford Edsel, a group of General Motors designers made a survey of what the typical *female* customer wanted in a motor car, and proceeded accordingly. After two years of research and the expenditure of eighty million dollars, the first Halicar Impala was built. The engine started well enough, but at 35 mph the linkage connecting the hair-drier to the eye-level grill snapped, disconnected the telephone, and threw the crib through the windscreen. Upon applying the brakes, the driver inadvertently set the instant heel-bar in motion, and was riveted to the wardrobe by a row of tintacks. A second Impala was never built.

IMPATIENS JINOTEGA

Jose Ortega "Impatiens" Jinotega was the father of modern bullfighting. Until his appearance in 1919, the average matador took eight hours to kill a bull, and there was only one fight per afternoon. Impatient as his nickname suggests, Jinotega soon saw that strangling was a slow and inept method, and, on his first appearance in the Barcelona ring, he pulled a sword from beneath his cloak, and despatched six fighting bulls in the space of half an hour. This book is a magnificent tribute to a man who died as he would have wished, gored by Ernest Hemingway during a bar-brawl in Pamplona.

JIRASEK LIGHTHOUSES

A penetrating analysis of the great Czech film director, Imry Jirasek, known in the West as Jirasek Lighthouses, after his greatest film, a four-hour satirical study of the life of a solitary wick-trimmer. *Lighthouses* was followed by *An Old Bus*, *Jackets*, and the deeply disturbing *My Bath And Hat*. After vigorous appeals by Ken Tynan, Arnold Wesker, Vanessa Redgrave, George Melly and others, Jirasek was allowed to leave Prague for England. He left London almost immediately for Hollywood, where he now makes half a million dollars a year scripting *I Love Lucy*.

LIGHTING MAXIMILIAN

Sean Kenny's detailed account of his special effects work on the Peter Weiss/Peter Brook production of *The Manic Depression And Concomitant Hallucinations That Led To The Nervous Breakdown Of Emperor Maximilian Of Austro-Hungary As Performed By Members Of The Portuguese World Cup Team.*

MAXIMINUS NAPLES

The first Proconsul of what was, in the second century BC, still Calabrium, Maximinus is chiefly remembered for his habit of throwing political opponents into Vesuvius. His proconsulate was exceptionally stormy, corrupt and inefficient, and in 134 BC, Emperior Tiberius Gracchus demoted him to the proconsulate of Sicilia, where he is chiefly remembered for his habit of throwing political opponents into Etna. His significance is minimal, and my own opinion is that this dreary account was long underdue.

NAPOLEON OZONOLYSIS

The story of how Napoleon Ozonolysis rose from humble origins to become the wealthiest Greek shipowner in the world has, of course, all the fabulous ingredients of legend, and in this frank autobiography (as told to Bobby Moore), the amazing tycoon reveals all. Lavishly illustrated with photographs of colonels, the book also contains an extremely useful index of eligible American widows. Just the thing for a Hellenic cruise, or a short piano leg.

P—PLASTERING

I opened this volume with considerable trepidation, believing it to be just another Do-It-Yourself tract. Imagine my delighted surprise to discover that it was in fact a history of stammering! Packed with fascinating information—did you know, for example, that George Washington was unable to enunciate "teaspoon," or that *K-K-K-Katie* was not written by Gustav Mahler?—the book is a veritable mine of glottal arcana. The appendix on Regency hiccups is on no account to be missed.

PLASTICS RAZIN

If you like escapology as much as I do, then you'll find it hard to resist this vivid biography of The Great Razin (pronounced *Rah'tsin*). Louis Razin's career began astoundingly early: in the last stages of labour, his mother was rushed to hospital in Boston, Mass, by hansom cab, but by the time she arrived on the maternity ward, she was no longer pregnant. Hysterical, she was led back to the waiting cab by her doctor, only to find the infant Louis screaming on the back seat! By the age of fourteen, he was already The Great Razin and Doris (subsequently The Great Razin and Beryl, after Doris had failed to emerge from a cabinet on the stage of the Holborn Empire), and in 1923 he became the first man to escape from a strait-jacket on radio. When transatlantic flights became regular with the advent of the Super Clipper, Razin celebrated by eating an entire canteen of airline cutlery, and the nickname stuck. Plastics Razin is buried in Boston Cemetery, probably.

RAZOR SCHURZ

On the afternoon of September 8, 1926, a short, stocky man in a barathea coat and a pearl-grey fedora walked into a garage in South Side Chicago. When he walked out again, four minutes later, he left six men dead behind him, cut to ribbons. That was the beginning of the career of Razor Schurz, dreaded torpedo of the Capone gang and by the time he was finally trapped in an alley beside the Rexo Bowling Palace in Peoria, Illinois, early in 1937, and mown down by the guns of J. Edgar Hoover—or was it the hoovers of J. Edgar Gun? The print in my copy was tiny and execrable—he had accounted for no less than sixty-eight other hoodlums. This book, by the way, is now being made into seven feature films.

SCHÜTZ SPEKE

Schütz speke (sometimes schützspeke) was an entirely new language invented by embittered ex-Esperantist Wilhelm Schütz, and was designed to be the greatest international medium of communication the world had ever known. Unfortunately, the secret died with Schütz, and since this volume is written in it, the publisher's motives escape me. It may be a tax-loss, or something.

SPELMAN TIMMINS

This expensively produced facsimile edition of the diary of a fourteenth-century warlock is not particularly interesting in itself, but it contains some interesting recipes entirely new to me: I would recommend in particular his tasty *langues de crapauds au fin bec*, even if it does, for some mysterious reason, make your face come out in long ginger hair.

TIMOLEON-VIETA

These collected love-letters of young Timoleon, Prince of Tyre, to Vieta, the beautiful fourteen-year-old daughter of a Sidonian lunatic, make poignant reading. The two lovers never touched, and saw one another only briefly, just once, when Timoleon's carriage ran down Vieta's milk-float early in 981 AD. Their tender and passionate affair came to an abrupt end when palace Nubians employed by Timoleon's tyrannical father seized the young prince and cut off his allowance.

VIETNAM ZWORYKIN

If, like me, you find the radical-chic posturings of the Zworykin family of New York extremely tiresome—tracts and polemica by Nat "Cuba" Zworykin, Sharon "Women's Lib" Zworykin, Chuck "Legalise Acid" Zworykin, Sigmund "Environment" Zworykin, and Dustin "Kill the Pigs" Zworykin have all become best-sellers on both sides of the Atlantic—then this new tirade by the youngest member, Willy "Vietnam" Zworykin, is not for you, despite its foreword by Gore Vidal, its addendum on Ulster by Edward Kennedy, its footnotes on the poor finish of the Side-winder missile by Ralph Nader, and its jacket-blurb by Jane Fonda. The fact that the whole text can be pulled out to form a banner may be of interest to bibliophiles.

Baby Talk, Keep Talking Baby Talk

Harvard's Social Psychiatry Laboratory has been analysing the special language adults use when talking to children; and it doesn't like it. Children, it believes, should be spoken to as adults. And vice versa?

The Savoy Grill. An elderly diner has pushed his plate to one side and is staring absently into the middle distance. To him, a waiter.

"You haven't eaten up your blanquette de veau, sir."

"I don't want it."

"Don't be a silly diner. It's delicious."

"It isn't."

"It is."

"Isn't!"

"Is!"

"ISN'T! ISN'T! ISN'T!"

"I'm going to turn my back, sir, and I'm going to count up to ten, and when I turn round again I want to see all that nice blanquette de veau eaten up. ONE—TWO—THREE—"

"I'm going to be sick."

"—FIVE—SIX—"

"I'm going to stick my fingers down my throat and I'm going to be sick on my new dinner jacket and I'm going to be sick on my new shoes and I'm going to be sick on my new mistress and I'm going to be sick on the tablecloth, and I *DON'T CARE!*"

"Look, sir, shall I tell you what we're going to do? You see that great big boiled potato? Well, that's Mount Everest. And the brussels sprouts are going to climb right up it."

"Why?"

"Because they're mountaineers."

"Why?"

"Because it's there."

"Why?"

"Because it is, and because I say so. But when they get to the top, they're going to be eaten by a Yeti. And do you know who the Yeti is?"

"No."

"You are, sir! You're a big brave Yeti, and you're going to eat all the mountaineers up!"

"I'm *not* a Yeti, I'm not, I'm *not*! I want some pudding."

"Sorry, sir, no pudding until you've eaten your blanquette de veau all up."

"I'll scream!"

"That's quite enough of that, sir. Do you want me to call the Head Waiter?"

"No."

"You know what the Head Waiter does to naughty diners, don't you, sir?"

"Yes."

"So you're going to eat up your nice blanquette de veau, aren't you?"

"Can I have some pudding afterwards?"

"If you're very, very good."

"All right."

The Manager's office, Barcloyd's Bank. A knock on the door.

"Yes? Ah—it's Hopcroft, isn't it?"

"Hoskins, sir."

"Speak up, boy!"

"*Hoskins*, sir!"

"Have you got something in your mouth, Hoskins?"

"It's a—no, sir—I mean, yes sir, it's my pipe, sir."

"And you think you can come in here smoking a pipe, do you, Hoskins? You think you can *afford* a pipe, do you?"

"Well, sir, I—"

"Don't lie to me, Hoskins, you snivelling little beast! And stop scratching yourself. What's that in your hand?"

118

"It's my m-monthly statement, sir."

"Is it, Hoskins, is it indeed? And are you proud of your monthly statement, Hoskins?"

"No, sir."

"No, sir. Well nor am I, sir. And I've asked you to come and see me, Hoskins, because I'm very disappointed in you. Very disappointed indeed!"

"I'm sorry, sir."

"Stop whining, Hoskins! If there's one thing I can't stand, it's a customer who whines. I had great hopes for you, Hoskins: I pride myself on being able to pick a promising customer, a customer who'll go far, a customer who will be a credit to Barcloyd's. A credit, Hoskins. Do you even know what the word means?"

"Yes, sir."

"I doubt that, Hoskins. I doubt that very much. You will please conjugate the verb *to be in credit.*"

"I am in credit, thou art in credit, he is in credit, we are in credit, you are in credit, they are in credit."

"And *are* you in credit, Hoskins?"

"No, sir."

"I despair, Hoskins, I truly despair. Look at the other customers, look at Sibley, and Greene, and Maltravers, look at Finnegan—credit accounts, deposit accounts, special accounts, joint accounts, all in credit, all improving every day, all rising to the top, all customers I can be proud of. And look at your younger brother, Hoskins Minor: he's just become Hoskins & Gribble Ltd. He'll go far."

"Yes, sir."

"Now, Hoskins, your teller informs me that you want to buy a bicycle. Is this true?"

"Well, sir, I thought—"

"I know what you thought, Hoskins, you thought you'd sneak off at every opportunity and go gallivanting about on your wretched machine instead of working. Well, Hoskins, I am not having it, do you hear? Now, unfortunately, our rules only permit me certain penalties, and since you are already paying eleven per cent on your wretched scroungings—God, if the Founder had lived to see a Barcloyd's chap beg!—there is only one other course open to me. You will stay behind after work, Hoskins, and you will do one hour's overtime per day. Is that clear?"

"Yes, sir."

"And think yourself lucky you live in so-called enlightened times, Hoskins. In my day, you'd have been hauled up in front of the whole bank and made bankrupt! Now get out!"

"Yes, sir. Thank you, sir."

A Surbiton bedroom. Afternoon. The blinds are drawn. The door bursts open.

"ALICE! You're playing with that awful milkman again! What did I tell you would happen if I ever caught you with him after last time?"

"You said you'd divorce me."

"And did I say I would never ever play with you again?"

"Yes."

"I only come up 'ere about the one doz large brown eggs as per note, I never—"

"You shut up! You just shut up! You're a nasty horrid person and we don't want you playing in our house! Alice is *my* friend!"

"I wasn't doing nothing, I was only talking, I didn't touch nothing, I never—"

"That's a double negative! You're a stupid uneducated little snot, and you live in a council estate, and you're not allowed to play with nice people! That was a double negative, Alice, did you hear it? That's what happens when you ask them in. You'll be picking up all sorts of things."

"He's not common, Reginald, he's not, he's NOT!"

"He's still got his socks on, Alice. He's in bed with his socks on!"

"So what?"

"Har, har, har! Who's in bed with his socks on? Har, har, har! You wait till I tell your mother about this, Alice, you wait till I tell her about him with his socks on in bed!"

120

"*Your* mother used to wear a wig! Reginald's mummy used to wear a ginger wig, Dennis!"

"Wun't surprise me. Wun't surprise me at all. Wun't—"

"You just shut up! Your feet smell."

"So do yours, with brass knobs on, and no returns."

"*And* you haven't folded your trousers! He hasn't folded his trousers, Alice, he's just thrown them down all anyhow, he's just thrown them on the floor! You've just thrown them on the floor, you horrible little bogie!"

"Knickers!"

"Horse stuff in the road!"

"Wee-wee!"

"There we are, Alice, he's swearing, he's saying filthy things, what did I tell you? Why are you playing with him?"

"It's your fault, Reginald, you won't play with me anymore, you're always going out or too tired or something, and he's got all sorts of new games, it serves you right, so there!"

"But he's not even a member of our *gang*, he's never played Conservatives in his life, he's got hairs in his nose, and—"

"If you let me in your gang, you can 'ave a go on the float."

"What? I mean, pardon?"

"You can drive it up Winchmore Crescent and back."

"Oh."

"You can blow the 'ooter and rattle the crates, and everything."

"Can I wear your cap?"

"Yes."

"And the satchel with the change in?"

"Yes."

"Super!"

"Can Dennis come to play again, then, Reginald?"

"Well—only if he's very, very good."

"He is."

"All right, then."

The Object Is Not Only Not To Win, It's Not Even To Take Part, Either—A Select List Of Christmas Games For Adults

Postman's Knock

This game is usually played throughout the Yuletide season, i.e. from about November 9 onwards. It also goes by the names of Dustman's Knock, Butcher's Knock, Newspaperboy's Knock, Grocer's Knock, and Remember-Me-I'm-The-Man - Who - Came - The - Year - Before - Last - To - Do - That-Outside-Drain-Of-Yours Knock. The rules are fairly simple: the householder waits in an upstairs room with the cutains drawn, peering through a chink; as soon as he sees one of the other contestants coming down the garden path (it is the first time since last Christmas that they have taken this route, having otherwise preferred the longer, but more picturesque trip via the azaleas, the newly-sown grass, and the lobelia bed), he rushes around the house switching off the lights, radios, etc. and locking such things as children and dogs in a sound-proof cupboard under the stairs. The Postman/Dustman/Andsoforth then knocks. After ten seconds he knocks again. After a further ten seconds, he pokes open the letterbox and cries: "Merrychristmasappynewyearguvnor!" The other player has to remain absolutely silent. If he makes a noise, he pays a forfeit (anything up to a fiver). If he remains silent, however, he pays a forfeit (anything up to a dustbin on his Rover).

Hunt The Slipper

Almost every family in the land will be playing this extremely popular game over the next few days. At some time during the seasonal junketing, the doorbell rings; the householder's wife goes to the door, and cries in a penetrating voice "HALLO AUNTIE RITA!" This is the signal for the householder to leap from his drunken glaze, race up the stairs, and begin rummaging through a large pile of tartan felt objects in a corner of his bedroom. He is trying to find the pair of slippers given him by Auntie Rita. This is not easy, since he has been given at least fourteen pairs of slippers, all of which he not only hates but has also managed to detach from their accompanying cards. This is a curious game: while the odds on his finding the correct pair and so winning the prize (of having Auntie Rita come in and stay until the cheap ruby port has run out and her funny hat has come down over one eye) should, mathematically, be fourteen-to-one, they turn out in practice to be something in the nature of four-thousand-to-one. No-one has succeeded in explaining this phenomenon, least of all those men one tends to find on the fringes of funerals, weeping uncontrollably over not having been invited to attend the reading of the will.

Hyde Park Corner

All of us, of course, played this game as children, or, rather, as pubescent teenagers. The adult version, however, has rather less necking. Basically, the house-holder's brother-in-law turns up at the householder's Christmas party (usually with an amusing electrical device wired invisibly to his right palm which knocks the fillings out of your teeth when you shake hands with him, and a blonde in fun-fur hotpants who subsequently does a strip and/or or is sick on the householder's bank-manager) and collects all the male guests in one corner of the room, leaving the women to stare at one another's clothes. The brother-in-law then tells an extremely interesting story lasting two hours about how he's just driven the Jag from Maidenhead to Hyde Park Corner in forty-one minutes and eleven-point-three seconds according to his Rolex chronometer, which was, by the way, the watch chosen by the Helsinki Olympics Committee and is guaranteed to one second per month, which is not bad for only four-hundred-and-seventy quid, is it, 'course that's the wholesale price I'm talking about. This game is over when the male guests, who happen to be the only friends the householder has in the world, start looking at their Timexes and their wives and drifting out into the night. The brother-in-law then collects his prize, which is usually about seven bottles of scotch.

Consequences

An extremely enjoyable game, this, particularly since it need not be restricted to the householder's own family circle, but may be extended almost infinitely. Nor is there any strict ruling on procedure: the game usually starts haphazardly, and just builds up. A typical example might begin with the householder giving his son an airgun, say, for Christmas; and the householder's neighbour giving *his* son a rabbit. The gun is used to shoot the rabbit, and the rabbit is used for shoving in the householder's face, on Boxing Day afternoon. The householder then withdraws the neighbour's invitation to the householder's booze-up, and the police join the game at midnight when the booze-up is at its height in pursuance of enquiries as to complaints laid under the My Wife And I Are Trying To Get Some Sleep Act, or some such. All the players then leave to be breathalysed, and the householder goes out and kicks the neighbour's fence down, after which the neighbour throws a brick at the householder's greenhouse. The game is over when the first For Sale placard appears.

Pig In The Middle

The householder sits at one end of a long table, his wife sits at the other, and eighteen morose relatives sit between them. The householder then takes a large roast animal and begins to carve until all the meat is off the bone; he then wraps his hand in bandages, and starts to carve the turkey. This having been at last accomplished, the thirty-six eyes of the other players leave him and follow the platter of meat as the householder's wife carries it around the table, and each player in the middle forks what he considers to be a decent portion onto his plate. The platter then returns to the householder, who eats the feet.

Musical Chairs

The game begins with eight comfortable chairs in the householder's living-room, and eight players sitting on them, including the householder. At this point, an elderly aunt belonging to the householder's wife turns up with her middle-aged bachelor son, unexpectedly. The householder gets up from his chair while the other players stare at him, and goes upstairs to get a chair from the bedroom and a stool from the bathroom. The object is to bring these two down together, not singly, thereby enabling the householder to gouge a track in the staircase wallpaper with the chair, and knock two banisters out with the stool. As soon as he arrives back in the living-room, the doorbell rings again, and he runs to open it, watched by the other players; to find his wife's cousin from Weybridge who was just passing through on his way to somewhere he *had* been invited, ha-ha-ha, and thought he'd drop in with the jolly old season's greetings. And his wife and her grandmother. The cousin and wife join the other players, leaving the householder to carry in the grandmother, who bites him under the impression something untoward is happening. When the householder gets to the living-room, all the players stare at him again. This time, he has to go up to the attic to get three folding chairs. As he is coming downstairs with these, they begin to unfold, skinning the householder's shins, and knocking off the top of the newel-post. This continues until the householder either runs out of chairs, or is taken away.

Statues

You will all have played this as children—one player has his

125

back to the rest, and when he turns they have to freeze in position—but it's much more fun in its adult version. Basically, the householder moves among his guests, chatting, filling glasses, and so forth, and obviously not able to keep an eye on everything. From time to time, however, he turns suddenly, and everyone stops: the object is to catch brothers-in-law nicking handfuls of cigars, pocketing half-bottles of gin, touching up the householder's wife (except in the case of blood relatives) and so forth. Anyone caught doing anything like this wins a poke in the mouth.

Simon Says

A favourite Christmas game for more competitive wives. Should the conversation turn to Red China, the devaluation of the dollar, private education, the escalating cost of Concorde, the Labour Party schism, or indeed anything else, Simon's wife (or Nigel's, or Roland's, or Henry's) interrupts with "Well, Simon says..." and proceeds to quote at length. Simon (or Nigel, or Roland, or Henry) takes no part in this game, he merely sits in the householder's favourite chair smiling his fatuous bloody smile and getting more and more smashed on the householder's single malt.

Ten Green Bottles

The householder's favourite Christmas game. When the party is in full swing, the householder goes out to the garden shed with a case of the best and stays there until about December 29th. There are no other players.

Me Aristocrat, You Jane!

**A report from America that anthropoid
apes were not just more intelligent than was
formerly supposed but might actually be
taught to speak a few simple phrases, opened
up vast areas of speculation. Since Edgar
Rice Burroughs was no longer around, I took
it upon myself to . . .**

A great stillness lay upon the shire. In the lush green thickets,
not a bird sang, not an insect rustled. In the dense copses, no
mammal moved, no reptile crawled. In the silver streams, the
trout lay leapless; and in the wild ponds, as in the ornamental
lakes, exotic mallards and alabaster swans alike tucked their
heads among their feathers, and drowsed. The very gnats hung
in the heavy air, motionless.

"Bloody good day, Sunday," murmured the Earl of Greystoke, turning in mid-snooze, and settling. The *Business
Observer* slid from his lap, softly, and lay, unread as ever, on the
velvet lawn. The other house-guests flexed slightly at his grunt,
and the faint creak of old basketwork echoed across the clearing: a few acres of greensward held by enormous effort against
the hungry foliage of Bucks., in the centre of which stood the
great peeling pile of Spiffins, the Greystoke seat.

They might, perhaps, have slumbered thus forever in that
close atmosphere, had not, at that very moment, a strange and
unsettling cry rung across the still countryside, an ear-shattering
"AAAAH-AAAAAH-AAAAAAH!" accompanied by the crash
of breaking branches and the odd counterpoint of rhythmic
thumping. The house-guests stirred, and sat up, and blinked at
the suddenly waving trees, as through them, a split-second later,

burst a short figure in black jacket, striped trousers, and Eton collar, swinging from limb to limb. Lithely, he dropped to the ground, and stared at them, suspicious as all small boys at the sight of visitors.

"My son, Lord Greystoke," said the Earl, and his heir hurtled up to shake the proffered hands. If any of the guests found it somewhat odd that Lord Greystoke's knuckles should be brushing the ground, or that the young Etonian should be sporting a thick black beard, they were, of course, far too well-bred to comment upon it; but one or two of the ladies with young but ultimately marriageable daughters could not entirely suppress a look of disappointment at his Lordship's extravagant bandiness. Too many gymkhanas, too early, they reflected. sighing; always a problem with country families.

They brightened, however, when Lord Greystoke snatched a sandwich from the waiting tea-trolley with his foot and popped it into his mouth.

"I say, that's jolly good!" cried a baronet.

"*Jolly* good!" exclaimed another. "Chap's an athlete!"

"Bags of spirit!" echoed a third. "How's his bowling?"

Lord Greystoke declined to comment. Instead, he was staring hard at the coiffure of the Dowager Duchess of Speenhamland, and baring his lips in a terrible grin.

"And what can I do for you, my little man?" she asked.

"I think he wants to examine your scalp," said the Earl.

His heir began jumping up and down enthusiastically.

"What fun!" cried the Dowager Duchess. She bent her head obligingly. Greystoke began to poke around on it.

"Enquiring mind," observed the Bishop of Bicester, nodding.

"Probably end up one of these scientist chappies," said a Viscount, "there's a lot of it about, I understand."

"Too deep for me, I'm afraid," said the Earl.

Everyone chuckled agreement. Satisfied, Lord Greystoke shot up an elm and began shaking its topmost branches.

"He's adopted, of course," said the Earl, as they watched his heir. "Parents worked in a circus, I believe. Good family, though. Truck overturned, killed 'em both, mile or so from here. Found the little lad wandering about in a daze. Took him in, brought him up as one of the family. Only thing to do."

"Bloody good show," said a baronet.

The ladies dabbed their eyes.

Lord Greystoke had a splendidly successful career at Eton. During his six years, he accumulated a dozen or so useful phrases (he was somewhat brighter than the average boy), and commended himself socially wherever he went, since he was anti-intellectual, enormously athletic, and had a way of looking at unpopular masters while bending a school railing between his bare hands that ensured an untroubled life for an understandably large number of close friends. He had also thrown the house bully through the library roof, and led his side to victory in the Wall Game for the first time in history, filling Slough General Hospital in the process.

Sexually, he remained something of a mystery. Once a month, he would go off to Whipsnade for the weekend and return looking happier and calmer; but, naturally, no-one ever pressed him on the subject. They were all, it must be remembered, members of the English upper classes, and stranger things had happened, even in the best-regulated houses.

It came as a surprise to none that, in his final year, Lord Greystoke became Head of Pop.

He failed to get into Oxford, despite the most benevolent-sounding Closed Scholarships, which was a source of tremendous relief to his father.

"Bloody good show!" said the Earl, when his son showed him the letter. "Thought for one ghastly minute you were turning into some kind of swot!"

"Rather not!" said Lord Greystoke, taking a banana from his monogrammed case and slipping it into his mouth, sideways.

"Bloody good!" said the Earl.

"Bloody good!" said Lord Greystoke. "Toppin'! Rippin'!"

"That's the kind of talk I like to hear!" cried his father. And got him into a good Guards' regiment.

Which was no mean feat, since Greystoke, though broad and muscular, was some two feet shorter than the requisite length of officer, and one or two voices could be heard muttering in the mess to the effect that they didn't know what England was coming to when the Ghurkas towered over a Coldstream; but money and influence prevailed, and, once in, Lord Greystoke again commended himself utterly to his peers, both professionally and socially, as well as, of course, intellectually. Within a fortnight, he had broken the collarbone of the Sergeant-Instructor, who looked on unarmed combat lessons as battles in the class-war, had placed a potty atop the Albert Memorial in the fantastic record time of fourteen seconds, and had beaten the Honourable Artillery Company's team at the Royal Tournament in the race to swing a twelve-pounder over a wall by tucking it, single-handed, under his left arm and grasping the rope in his right.

Furthermore, he turned out to be wonderful with animals. Every morning, as the dawn mists were melting in Hyde Park, he could be seen leading not only the Regiment's horses but also their dogs and the neighbourhood squirrels through the most complex and stirring manoeuvres. He seemed, uncannily, to speak their language.

The regimental goat loved him like a brother.

Evenfurthermore, his success at regimental dances, hunt balls, coming-out parties, and the like, was unparalleled! The life and soul of every party, he was wont not only to swing from the chandeliers of the Dorchester or the Grosvenor and lay out the waiters with magnums of Bollinger hurled as easily as if they had been coconuts, he had also been responsible for incinerating Annabel's and throwing The Who into the Serpentine.

He tended, inevitably, to smell a bit when hot.

In short, Lord Greystoke was everything that an officer and gentleman should be.

"What about the Stock Exchange?" said the Earl, when his son returned to civilian life.

"Bloody good," said Lord Greystoke.

"Or Lloyd's?"

"Or Lloyd's," said Lord Greystoke. "Bloody good."

So he deposited his hundred thousand; and had a job. His title also qualified him for three dozen assorted directorships—he was, of course, required to turn up at board meetings once a year to say "Bloody good!" and collect his salary—and as he had also lent his cachet to a new discotheque, a chain of boutiques for the shorter man, and a trendy treetop restaurant in Cheyne Walk, he was not only one of the richest young men about town, he was also one of the most eligible. True, he had an unfortunate habit of ramming bollards with a succession of Lamborghinis (his feet being unable to reach the brake), but this only served further to consolidate his growing reputation as wag, wit and playboy.

It was at a party at Antonia Fraser's to celebrate the opening of his first photographic exhibition that Lord Greystoke, as he was bound to do, fell in love.

It was a perfect match; everyone said so. The most eligible peer in England and the daughter of a world-wide grocery chain that had never turned in an annual dividend of less than twenty per cent.

" 'Andsome he ain't," said the world-wide grocery chain as he watched the couple descend the steps of Brompton Oratory, "but he ain't 'alf got tone."

"Right," said his wife. "And you can't buy that, can you?"

The world-wide grocery chain smiled. "I just 'ave," he said.

But when the happy couple returned from their Acapulco honeymoon, it could be discerned that the broad smile on the face of Lord Greystoke was not mirrored in the pale and haggard countenance of his lovely bride. Indeed, hardly had they touched down and Lord Greystoke gone off for a quiet scratch, than Lady Greystoke ran sobbing to her mother.

Who listened, for a long time, to a tale too bizarre even to be as exciting as it had promised; and said, when the final stillness came:

"Well?"

Which wasn't the sort of advice Lady Greystoke was after at all.

"What shall I *do*, Mumsy?" she said.

"Do?" said her mother. "You'll 'ave to get used to it, won't you? Think of your dad and me. They're asking us everywhere."

"But—"

"But bleeding nothing! What you don't understand, my girl, is 'e's an aristocrat. They're diff'rent, 'n'they?"

"Not 'alf."

"So you'll just 'ave to grin and bear it, won't you?"

So she did.

Boom, What Makes My House Go Boom?

**"One of the effects of the house-price spiral
and the rush to buy has been that estate
agents no longer find it necessary to disguise
the truth about their properties."** *The Observer*

I met him at the gate, as arranged. We looked up at the house together. He glanced at his watch, not unobviously.

"It's rather nice," I said. "I've always wanted to live in St. Johns Wood."

"No point going in, then," said the agent, taking a cigarette from his packet and deftly avoiding my reaching hand. "This is Kilburn."

"Oh, surely not! I understood that this area was traditionally described as, well, as St. Johns Wood borders?"

He sucked his teeth. He shook his head.

"Not even Swiss Cottage," he said. "Not even *West* Swiss Cottage."

"Swiss Cottage borders?" I begged.

"Kilburn." He put the watch to his ear. "If that."

"Oh."

"What do you expect," he muttered, "for twenty-three-nine-fifty?"

"Twenty-two-five," I corrected. I showed him the specification sheet.

He tapped it with a finger.

"Got yesterday's date on," he said.

"I received it this morning," I said, "and surely—"

"Lucky we sent it express," he said. "Might be out of your range tomorrow."

"Could we go in?" I enquired. "It's rather chilly here."

"What do you think it is inside?" he said. "Bermuda?"

"The central heating must make a—"

"*Part* central heating," he said. "Plus small boiler, totally inadequate to the job. Especially bearing in mind the lack of double-glazing. The only way to tell if the radiators are on is to put your cheek up against them and wait for a minute or two. Still, at twenty-four-two-fifty, you can't really complain, can you?"

"I suppose not," I said, "these town houses are at a premium these days."

"*Terraced* houses."

"I always thought—"

"Call a spade a spade, that's our motto. When you've got a long line of nondescript jerry-built bogus-regency items leaning on one another to keep from falling down, they're known as terraced houses. Or, in some cases, back-to-backs. If the gardens are as tiny as this one is." He opened the front door. "Don't rush in," he said, "or you'll miss it, ha-ha-ha!"

"Ha-ha-ha!"

"See that crack in the hall ceiling? You'd think they'd take a bit more care with a twenty-six-grand property, wouldn't you?"

"It doesn't look too bad," I said, "probably just a fault in the plastering. A good workman could fill that in in two shakes of—"

"That's what the previous owner thought," said the agent, stubbing his cigarette out on the wallpaper. "His dog fell through it and broke its neck. Treacherous, these stone floors."

"But sound," I said. "No chance of warp, dry rot, that sort of—"

"You wait till your plumbing packs up," he said. "Main conduit's under there: one day your bath's cold, the next you've got six blokes and a pneumatic drill poking about in your foundations. Want to see the kitchenette?"

"Thank you."

"'Course," he said over his shoulder as he forced the door,

"when I say foundations, that's only my little joke. Three inches of builders' rubbish and a couple of two-by-fours, and that's it. I wouldn't like to be here when the motorway goes through —one articulated truck, and you're liable to find yourself with half the roof in the downstairs lav."

"Oh, I didn't realise there was a downstairs lavatory," I said. "That's rather encourag—"

"I wouldn't show it to you," he said, "I wouldn't even talk about it. Not so soon after breakfast. This is the kitchenette."

"Kitchen*ette*?" I said. "Mind you, I suppose it is a bit on the small side, but—"

"*Small?* It's lucky there's no mice here, otherwise you'd have to take turns going to the larder."

"Well, you wouldn't expect mice in a modern house, would you?"

"Right. Rats yes, mice no."

"Oh. Well, we've got a cat, so—"

"That's one bedroom out for a start, then," he said. "Big cat, is it?"

"Neutered tom," I said.

The agent pursed his lips.

"Probably have to give him the master suite, in that case," he said. "At least he can shove open the bathroom door and stick his tail in if he starts feeling claustrophobic. Lucky it's on the first floor, really."

"I'm sorry?"

"If the cat's on the first floor, you and the family can sleep above it. On the second. You don't want a bloody great moggy stamping around overhead all night, do you? Let alone watching you and the missus through the gaps in the floorboards. Lying on your back listening to the tubes rumbling underneath, with a bloody great green eye staring down at you."

We left the kitchen, and came back into the hall. He opened another door.

"I imagine that's the dining-room?" I said.

"That's what you want to do, squire," he said. "Imagine. Mind you, it'd do for buffet suppers, provided the four of you all had small plates. The other door leads to the integral garage, by the way, if you were wondering what the smell of petrol was. You've got a car, I take it?"

"Yes."

"Don't forget to leave it outside, then. Bloke two doors down made the mistake of changing his Fiat 500 in for a Mini. Brought it home from the showroom, drove straight in, had to spend the night there. Wife fed him through the quarter-light. I suppose you could always have a sunshine-roof fitted, though."

"We'll leave ours out," I said. "It's more convenient, what with taking the kids to school every morn—"

"Oh, you won't need the motor for that, squire! School's only a stone's throw away."

"Really? Well, that's a load off—"

"Very good glazier up the road, though. Mind you, you have to take the day off to let him in. He won't come out at night."

"That's surprising."

"In this neighbourhood? After dark even the police cars cruise in pairs."

"Do you think we might go upstairs?"

"And that's only if there's a full moon."

"Four bedrooms, I think you said?"

"Well, three really. The third one's been split into two with a party wall, but you could easily convert it back. Just slam the front door, and bob's your uncle."

I started up the staircase, and it wasn't until I'd reached the first landing that I realised I was alone. The agent called up.

"You all right?"

"Yes," I shouted.

He joined me.

"Hope you don't mind," he said. "Never tell with these stairs. I reckoned you were about my weight." He patted the banister lovingly. "See that workmanship? They don't make 'em like that any more!"

"It's certainly an attrac—"

"Not after *Rex* v. *Newsomes Natty Fittings Ltd.*, they don't.

Christ!" he exclaimed, looking at his watch again. "It's never twelve o'clock already!"

"Two minutes past, actually."

"That's another half-hour off the lease, then." He turned, and started down the stairs again, gingerly. "I trust you have the requisite used notes in the motor, squire?"

I followed him down.

"I'd like a little time to think about it," I said, "and then, of course, my solicitor will have to make the necessary searches and—"

He laid a kindly claw on my arm.

"Do yourself a favour, son," he said gently. "Forget about searches. Tatty old drum like this, you can never tell what they might find. Now, look, am I going to be able to unload this or not?"

"Well, I'm not entirely certain, but—"

The agent wrenched open the front door. A queue stretched down the path, and into the street. Mute supplication blinked in their watery eyes.

"Says he's not certain!" cried the agent.

Instantly, the queue dismembered itself into a shrieking mob.

"One at a time!" yelled the agent, tearing a brassette carriage-lamp from the wall and beating a clearing among the grabbing throng. "Let's do this proper! Now, I am not asking twenty-nine-five for this mouldering pile! I am not asking thirty-two-and-a-half, all I'm asking is—"

I edged through the pitiful clamour, and out into the road, and bent my steps towards the YMCA. It's warm there, and there's a nice peg for your anorak and a shelf for your clock, and it'll be weeks before the developers start bidding for the site.

With luck.

A Life On The Rolling Mane

**"The National Federation of Hairdressers
has pledged itself to stamp out what it calls
Pirate Barbers."** *The Guardian*

I take up my pen in the year of grace 197–, and go back to the
time when my father kept the Maison Benbow Gents Salon and
the brown old barber with the razor scar first hove to under
our roof.

I remember him as if it were yesterday, as he came plodding
in beneath our creaking pole and threw himself thankfully into
the Number One chair, calling for a glass of our best bay rum.
A man who had seen better times, he was topped now with an
ill-fitting Fortescue Hairette wig; his once-natty pencil mous-
tache was nicotine-stained and asymmetrical, his nose-hairs
blew unplucked in the fan-breeze, and his fine chin was a-
pimple from the myriad nicks of a thousand unhoned blades.
But, from the black and broken nails, and the tufts of hair that
spilled from his turnups, and his habit of flicking himself, as
he sat, with a greasy grey tea-towel, I could tell that here was
a master barber of the old school.

He grasped the bay rum from my hand and tossed it back
with a single action, massaging it into his dewigged dome with
a free hand and a grateful sigh.

"Ah, that were good, laddie!" he cried. "Just the thing for
an ole barberman on a cole morning! What be the name on ye,
boy?"

"Jim, sir," I said. "Jim Hawkins."

He settled back, and closed his eyes.

"I see Huddersfield lost again, Jim," he murmured.

"Aye, sir," said I, "but what do 'ee think of the Common Market, then?"

"Nobbut bad'll come of 'er, Jim lad," he said. "But I likes the look o' the new Morris Minor."

"Put your money on Fair Folly," said I. "White City, eight o'clock."

"Warm for the time o' year," he answered. He sighed. "It's good to talk to a barberin' man again, Jim. Give us another bay rum, and put a drop o' summat in her, if you know what I mean, heh-heh-heh!"

I spiked his glass with a dash of friction rub, and his old eyes lit up.

"Ye've the makings of a master barber, Jim," said he. "I were a young shampoo boy meself once, Jim, proud, ambitious —not that ye'd reckon it, to look at me now. I seen 'ard times, Jim. Ye'd never think I was once master o' me own shop, a fine three-chairer, backwash basins gleaming like a virgin's teeth, a fine head o' steam in the ole steriliser and them new steel combs a-bobbin' . . ."

"Wonderful," said I, "I wouldn't give tuppence for Ted Heath's chances."

"Traffic's terrible this morning," said he. "Aye, three chairs and used to manufacture my own 'air-oil, too. Master of the brilliantine *Morning Rose*, that was yours truly, Jim."

"The *Morning Rose!*" I cried.

"You'm 'eard of her, then?" said he.

"Who hasn't?" I watched his face grow sad a thousand times in the swinging mirrors. "But what happened?" I asked.

"I got took!" he muttered bitterly. Suddenly, he swung round. "Watch out for a hairfaring man wi' one leg, Jim! Make sure yer shutters is locked tight a-nights! Keep a good razor by 'ee and doan ever—*what's that?*"

I listened, as he half-rose from the chair, and I heard it, too. Tap-tap-tap. Tap-tap-tap.

" 'Tis Bald Pew!" screamed the old barber. He turned, and his trembling finger pointed. There, at the point where the frosted glass of my father's shopfront joined the clear glass above, came slowly a seemingly disembodied white dome, like a huge darning mushroom. We could not see the face beneath, that moved, an eery shadow, along the frosting, nor the thing that tapped his creeping progress.

The old barber grasped my arm.

"That be his tail-comb, Jim!" he hissed. "A turrible thing! I seen Bald Pew kill three customers wi' that sharpened tail of his, just on account of them not wanting a two-bob singe!"

And, flinging the sheet from his throat, he was out of the chair in a trice, and gone! So intent was I thereafter in staring at the livid dome that had paused outside, I did not notice the new figure who had suddenly materialised in the doorway. When he spoke, I jumped for my life.

"Ahar, Jim lad!" he cried, and I looked, and I saw, and a cold sweat broke out upon my brow. It was he! He stood there, resting on his mahogany leg, a twisted smile upon his evil lip, and a mangy parrot coughing on his shoulder. I cannot say how long I stood in silence; but, at last, I unfroze my limbs.

"H-how do you know my name?" I asked.

He grinned a horrible grin, and swung himself into the shop.

"I make enquiries, Jim lad, doan I? I knows where the best shampoo boys is to be found, heh-heh! Silver's the name, Jim, Cap'n Silver, on account of what the customers 'as to cross my palm with, if they doan want to carry 'ome their ears in a cardboard box, heh-heh-heh!" He nodded his great head towards the parrot. "And this here's Cap'n Skint."

"*Will there be anything else, sir?*" shrieked the parrot. "*Will there be anything else?*"

"Got 'im nice and trained, ain't I, Jim?" cried Silver. He stumped closer. "Like all my bonny boys," he cackled. A great hand fell on my shoulder. "I come for 'ee, Jim lad! 'Tis a great opportunity for a boy!"

I turned, such was my innocence, to indicate the shop.

"But I have a position, sir, and I do not wish—"

I got no further. I felt a terrible blow upon my head, and a deep blackness rose inside me, and I knew no more.

It was the jolting that awoke me. Wherever I was, it was moving. I opened my eyes, and found myself—in a barber's shop! But such a barber's shop as I had never looked upon: small, filthy, its mirrors cracked and yellowed, its walls hung with tattered magazines of a like no Christian man could look upon unblushing. Rickety cabinets held objects I had never before set eyes on, strange oils and unguents and packages, and little booklets bound in cellophane. Two old bentwood chairs had been nailed to the floor, and two galvanised pails clanged from wallnails in front of them. Three of the most villainous looking men I have ever seen sat on a chest at one end, drinking from a jug. One lacked an ear, another an eye, the third had but six fingers. And then I heard the dread voice of Silver.

"I see you'm lookin' over the staff, Jim lad!" he roared. "Ain't they as pretty a bunch as you ever did clap yer lights on, heh-heh-heh! They got that way from practisin', Jim. I likes 'em to keep their 'ands in, doan I, when business is slack?"

"*Will there be anything else, sir?*" screamed Captain Skint. "*Will there be anything else?*"

"What does that mean, sir?" I asked.

The staff laughed horribly, nudging one another, and rolling with the motion of the shop.

"There's a lot ye got to learn about the good shop *Hispaniola*, Jim lad!" cried Silver. "But Long John'll teach 'ee, woan I?"

"Why are we moving?" said I.

"We'm aboard a mobile salon, Jim," said he, "bound for the rich pickings of Morplesden Tradin' Estate. 'Course, to the casual eye, we'm just an artickilated removal van, ain't we, till we strikes our colours, heh-heh. *Belay there!*"

At his bellow, the crew, who had begun picking one another's scalps, sprang apart.

"Alopecia, Jim," explained Silver. "Drives 'em mad, sometimes. That and the dermatitis. 'Tis the freebooter's curse, Jim. But doan ever let me catch 'ee scratchin' in front o' the customers, Jim, or I'll 'ave yer tongue for stropping. Likewise peeing in they pails: if I hears that tinkling in the middle o' the night,

I'll know what to do, woan I, lads? We'm turned more'n one promising baritone into a boy soprano, ain't we, heh-heh-heh!"

I shuddered, but the grace of God saved me from further vile reflection, for at that very moment there came a great shout from up for'ard.

"Customers onna starboard bow!"

Silver sprang to his foot, and slid back the hatchway separating the salon from the helmsman's cabin. In the tiny rectangle, I could see the serried alloy roofs winking in the spring sun, and my nostrils caught the fresh tang of light industrial air. With a shout of joy, Silver snatched an old scrap of AA book from his pocket and stabbed his filthy finger at it.

" 'Tis Morplesden, me hearties! Rich pickings, and nary a landlubbing coiffeur for twenty mile! Full ahead, Mister MacSwine, and strike the colours!"

The great salon yawed, rattling the jars and bottles, and swung off the main lane and down a little gravelly creek, as the crew poked open a hatch in the roof and ran up the barber's pole and the three Open-For-Business flags. Within minutes, we had dropped anchor, and the crew were swarming to the tailboard gunwale. Silver grabbed a weapon from its hook, and rubbed the dandruff from it with a filthy cloth. He clicked it once or twice beneath my nose.

"Remember the days of the great clippers, Jim!" he cried, his mad eyes blazing. "No, 'course you don't, young sprat like 'ee! Werl, there's no electrics aboard the *Hispaniola*, lad, and ye can lay to that! Craftsmen, ain't we, me hearties?"

The vile crew cheered through the scissors clenched in their ochre teeth. Silver banged his peg-leg against the tail-board.

"Lower a cutter!" he cried.

One of the men stepped forward, brandishing his scissors, leapt ashore, and made off towards the colony at a brisk trot. Within minutes, he reappeared, leading a column of hirsute dots.

"Stand by to fleece boarders!" cried Silver. "And just 'ee remember, not a man-jack of 'em as goes back wi'out restyling, blow waves, shave, shampoo, singe, manicure, pedicure, 'ot towels, and a large carton of anything else, if 'ee doan want to end up in Maison Davy Jones, heh-heh-heh!"

As the thin line of innocent natives approached the *Hispaniola*, a shaving-mug was thrust into my hand.

"Get a-latherin', Jim lad!" cried Silver. "I wants it slapped on 'em as they step aboard, doan I, afore they 'as time to say no. Good gobful of foamy Sunlight allus keeps 'em quiet fer a bit, and—*hell fire and damnation!*"

He sprang back, whipping a cut-throat from his belt, and as he cleared the light I saw an orange minivan come streaking towards us, honking its horn, and flashing its bow lights!

" 'Tis Sanitary Inspecker Trelawney, lads!" roared Silver, and at his cry the crew sprang back from the tail-board and began hauling down our colours. The cutter broke into a sprint, leaving the bewildered natives, and flung himself over our stern.

"Up anchor!" screamed Silver, "'Tis six months wi'out the option, this time!"

And before I could prepare myself, the great salon lurched from her moorings, hurling me over the stern, and onto the verge! When I recovered my senses, the *Hispaniola* was no more than a distant speck on the shimmering horizon.

I never saw her again.

Nor never shall. Oxen and wain-ropes would not bring me back again to that accursed spot; and the worst dreams that I ever have are when I hear the boom of the scurf, or start upright in my bed with the sharp voice of Captain Skint still ringing in my ears: "*Will there be anything else, sir? Will there be anything else?*"

The Night We Went To Epernay By Way Of Tours-sur-Marne

This is Fère-en-Tardenois. I'm damned glad I only have to write it down. I'd hate to have to try saying it. Not that I couldn't, all other things being, you know. I said it a lot this afternoon. I have a great French accent, sober.

That doesn't mean I can't hold it. It's just, we had a lot of bottles today. I'm a scotch drinker, normally, you understand. And you wouldn't believe the number of people I've seen off. Some of the world's most outstanding soaks. Just stood there while they slid to the ground, poured myself a nightcap, walked away straight as a plank. Ask anyone.

I don't think I ever drank eight bottles of champagne in a day before, though. I've just noticed that I started a sentence with a conjunction a few inches back, in case you're interested. They tried to knock that out of me at school. Nobody cared about style in the early 'fifties.

Any minute the people in the room next door are going to start banging on the walls. You know the French; a volatile folk. Man starts typing at three in the morning, they can get very upset, pretty soon this bedroom is going to be full of waving arms. I wonder if they have a hotel detective? What do you say to Rupert Davies at three in the morning?

Still, they're luckier than the people downstairs. They've been waiting since one-fifteen for me to drop the other shoe. I really would, you know me, not a spark of malice in my entire make-up, it's just that it has laces, and you know what laces are like if you have eleven thumbs. I pulled the other one off. Not thumb, the other shoe. But that was a long time ago, and I don't seem to have any energy left.

I'd write longhand if I could, but the pen's in my jacket, and my wife is asleep on it, and when I tried to get my cigarette lighter out of the pocket a little while back, she went for me with her teeth. I've never seen her do that before. Maybe she isn't a champagne drinker, either.

Can you get rabies off people?

I rang down for room service a few minutes ago. I woke up, and the bathwater was freezing, and when I saw all the earwigs floating round me, I nearly had a heart attack. I couldn't move. I thought, there's enough earwigs there to eat an entire man, e.g. me, and then I thought, I won't show them I'm afraid, they smell fear, earwigs, so I started whistling, very slowly. And then I saw they weren't earwigs at all, they were shreds of tobacco, my cigarette must have come apart while I was asleep. I was certain when I saw a cork tip come past. I may be drunk, but there's no insect looks like a cork tip, that I do know.

So I got out of the bath, and

That must be the reason I can't get the other shoe off. It's either the leather has shrunk, or the laces. I hope to God whatever it is dries out to its normal size. I don't want to spend the rest of my life in this black shoe.

So I got out of the bath, and I rang room service, and asked for a bottle of Perrier, because while I was asleep someone had come in and carpeted my throat, and Room Service said: "Entendu, m'sieu" and then he came up, and this is a very expensive hotel and you would expect an employé of same not to stand in the doorway with his bouche hanging there in neutral, and I said to him:

"What's the matter, didn't you ever see anyone with a shoe on before?"

and he snapped out of it, and opened the Perrier, and didn't even wait for a tip, which was just as well, since the money was under my wife, still is, along with the pen and the lighter, and there could have been a nasty scene and who knows what the penalty might be under the Code Napoleon for biting a waiter going about his lawful duties?

The thing is, I could be wrong, but I think the Perrier is

making me drunk again. I think it's getting together with all that dormant champagne, and I think they're cooking something up.

It's been a long day. I've had months that were shorter. It all started peacefully enough, we were coasting down Route Nationale 31, I think it was, one of those undifferentiated cobbly ribbons rimmed with white cows that the French seem to go in for, and the next moment we turned south at Fismes, and there it all was. It isn't every day that you breast a slight rise to find an entire national character suddenly at your feet. On, as it were, the hoof. There it all was, slope after slope of little brown vine-frames, a billion buds-worth of the '74 vintage awaiting its turn to be converted into christenings, wakes, seductions, ship-launchings, motorway-openings, anniversaries, celebrations, commiserations, and just plain booze-ups. Thirty thousand acres of embryo burps, giggles, hangovers, and blokes walking into walls in the small hours.

It is this, the sheer *concentration* of Champagne, that first makes the imagination reel and grope: a mere thirty thousand acres to serve the world. Call for a bottle on the Ginza, snap your fingers in El Vino, pop a cork in Valparaiso or Durban or Tunbridge Wells, and the stuff that pricks the nostril and galvanises the soul started off somewhere in these few square kilometres, as a pip.

It would be hard to think of another tiny patch of the globe's surface so rife with overtone, so alive to its own symbolism, and so much the quintessence of its host race. Here is the nub and concentrate of all things Gallic. As if there were a town called Tea, say, just off the M4, from which the whole essence of England emanated; as if there were Coke, Nebraska, or Guinness, Co. Cork.

We took the road to, my God an owl's just gone off on the window-sill, we took the road to Hautvillers, that sweet shrine above the Marne where Dom Pérignon spent a large slice of the seventeenth century in glorifying God in an approved Benedictine manner, i.e. by jumping up and down on the fruit of the vine until these products of the Almighty's grand design had been improved beyond all recognition, a heresy upon which successive Popes were prepared to turn a conveniently blind eye, especially in a good year. True believers owe the good monk much: apart from his years of unflagging basement service in tasting and blending, Dom Pérignon also found time to invent the cork. Without it, champagne could never have been, relying as it does upon that little spongy cylinder for the extraction of its sedimentary gunge, and the retention of its bubble.

So we drank a morning bottle to old Dom, and the stuff fizzed in its two cones like pale liquescent gold, and the sun came out over the Marne, and I think, now I remember, there were larks, too. And we drove down to Epernay, across the river, singing, into the commercial heartland of Champagne, down streets called Moet and Perrier and Chandon, a map like a Temperance Union itinerary of hell, little alleys behind the high old walls of which the faithful clerks with paper cuffs made out the lading-bills to Tokyo and Bonn and Manchester; and the trucks passed by us, bearing the brut to the English, and the doux to the East, and allsorts to the Americans, who like to drink it so cold that it wouldn't matter if it was carbonated wood-alcohol, anyway, and we dropped in at Les Berceaux and we had another bottle there, and that was even better than the first, and there were yet fewer clouds when we came out again; so we put the hood down, and we sang more loudly still, and drove back over the Marne, and up to Rheims, because the good people of Heidsieck & Co. Monopole had asked us to lunch, and Rheims is where they hang their hat.

Was it only a dozen hours ago?

They took us down into the cool vaults, where there are eight miles of corridors hewn out of that same chalk that nourishes the vine, and these eight miles have a strange mould for décor, like a green flock wallpaper, and ten million bottles for furniture, and it all reeks of vinous age; and men in blue dungarees walk through, at measured pace, ritually, and turn each bottle with a single deft and wristy move; forty men turning three thousand bottles an hour, for all eternity, so that the sediment has no inimical peace.

We went aloft again, leaving the ten million bottles to their restlessness. How can I express ten million bottles in terms you'll comprehend? Perhaps it would be simpler to think of it as slightly more than two million bottles each for every man, woman and child in my family.

Upstairs, we drank two bottles more, of their finest cuéve, and it is none of your NV stuff to make the bridesmaids giggle, but a very fine wine indeed, and there was more at lunch, at the Heidsieck windmill high on a green hill at Verzenay. My host took me to the window, and remarked that the old Moulin had been an allied observation post in both World Wars, and I peered, and tried to observe what the allies had observed, only by that time I was having difficulty seeing as far as the host.

And we left them in the mild afternoon, and we said to one another How do you top that? but there was a spot we had heard of called Le Château de Fère-en-Tardenois, and top it it did, no disrespect to the Moulin: a castle on a moated mountain, built in the thirteenth century and falling down ever since, due, claim its curators, merely to the ravages of time, but I have my doubts. I lay blame at the cuisine at its foot, at the Hostellerie du Château, where the food is so superb and the booze so prime, that when the last draught of marc and coffee has been sunk, one wanders out into the soft evening and up to the castle ruins, and, in one's euphoria, tends to bump into the hallowed reliquiae with never a second thought. There's a sliver of crenellation in my shoe right now; the way things are, it may stay there for good. I am living history.

The dawn is doing things now. The birds are crazed. The sun is poised to warm the grape-buds out there beyond the ruins. There must be a hundred million bottles of the stuff in the immediate vicinity.

I may stay here forever. If I can find my other shoe.

The Hounds Of Spring Are On Winter's Traces, So That's Thirty-Eight-Pounds-Forty, Plus Making Good, Say Fifty Quid

This is the week, according to my much-thumbed copy of *Milly-Molly-Mandy Slips A Disc*, when Winter officially knocks off for a few days, the swallows return from Africa to foul the greenhouse roof, and you and I be a-diggin' and a-stretchin' and a-sweatin' as we work away with that most indispensable of gardening tools, the wallet.

And, as no newspaper or magazine is currently worth its salt without a few inches of pithy advice to the dehibernating gardener, it has fallen to my lot to deliver this year's handy hints. And if you think a sentence containing both salt and lot has been cobbled together as a subtle augury of the doom lying just beyond the french windows, then you might as well stop reading immediately: anyone who has time to work out textual cruces of that convoluted order clearly has nothing more effortful to bother about than a window box with a plastic begonia cemented to it. This piece is for committed gardeners only; although those who have not yet been committed may, of course, read it while waiting for the ambulance.

Fences

This is the time of year to get together with your neighbour over the question of repairs to fences, trellises, and so on, that have deteriorated or even collapsed during the winter. I have always found that the best implement for dealing with this problem is a small hammer. If you have a large neighbour, then take a large hammer.

Blackwood

Similar to the above, and particularly satisfying for bridge-players. You creosote your fencing somewhat enthusiastically, with the result that your neighbour's herbaceous border drops dead. He then digs a large trench on his side, until light shows between the soil and your new fencing. This is known as the Small Spade Opening. The conventional reply is Two Clubs.

Corm, Bulb, Tuber and Rhizome

Not, of course, the long-established firm of country solicitors they might appear to the uninitiated, but the business end of those perennial plants which we gardeners carefully took up at the first sign of winter. At the first sign of spring, take them carefully out of their boxes and throw them away.

Exactly why all perennial roots die during the winter is an issue on which botanical opinion has long been divided: many experts argue that those stored in garages have an adverse reaction to being run over, and that this, coupled with the frost coming through the window the sack fell off in October and that nobody's wife got around to putting back up, explains why so many bulbs go flat and black during the weeks immediately prior to replanting.

Many other things, however, can carry off the apparently healthy corm, e.g. dogs, children, dailies with empty tubs at home, but since the plants will be dead anyway, these do not call for the hammer treatment.

Things like Geraniums

Now is the time to go and look at the things like geraniums which you left in the ground all winter, knowing that if you lifted them, potted them, and stored them the way the books recommend, they would all die of mould. Left in the ground, they die anyway but at least you don't break your nails. If they haven't died in the ground, they are not geraniums but merely things and your best bet is to burn them off with a blow-lamp (see below under BLOW-LAMP) because otherwise they will take over the entire garden by March 23.

Blow-lamp

Now is the time to take down your blow-lamp and run. Because of an extremely complicated chemical process it would take far too long to elaborate upon, much gets up blow-lamp spouts between Michaelmas and yesterday morning. When you attempt to prime and light the blow-lamp, it ignites your suit. The way to avoid this happening is called £3.95.

Motor Mower

The motor mower is exactly similar to the blow-lamp in principle, but rather more sophisticated, which means that after it ignites your suit, it takes your fingers off at the knuckle as well. The best thing to do is call in an expert, but make sure you phone before April 3, 1948, as they get pretty booked up at this time of year. You can always use a HAND MOWER if you want to lose the entire hand. This comes about through trying to remove last year's long grass which has become wound round the axle and, by an extremely complicated chemical process it would take far too long to elaborate upon, turned to iron. Again, there is a traditional country remedy for both these problems and your bank manager would be pleased to advise you.

Lawns

Now you have your new lawn-mower, you will want to get something to cut, since all lawns are annual. A few tufts here and there may have survived the winter, but upon closer inspection these will turn out to be clumps of clover, saw-grass, couch-grass, and the cat. What your lawn needs now is feeding and planting. Many people ask me how I achieve a lawn like a billiard-table, i.e. no grass anywhere and full of holes, and I usually recommend any one of a dozen products now on the market in which various chemicals have been carefully blended to ensure that you will be back next year

151

to try again. If you read the labels on these products, you will see that they may not be used either after it has rained or before it is due to rain, thus protecting the manufacturers from complaints lodged by anyone other than an astrologer with his eye in. Sprinkle these on the grass, watch them blow onto the roses, dig up and burn the roses, wait two days for the grass to be eaten away, dig over, pave, and sell the mower back. You can, of course, avoid this costly process by using lawn sand, a preparation used by experts wishing to turn lawn into sand, and there is much to be said for having a nice stretch of beach between your fences: put up an umbrella, a couple of deckchairs, and an electric fire on a long lead, and you could be in Baffin Land.

Manure

Now is the time of year when you will want to think about top-dressing your rose-beds, and why not? There's no harm in thinking. Many people, it seems to me, worry far too much about finding true horse manure, when the commercial preparations available are just as good, bearing in mind that by the time you get them off the shovel, the roses have already begun to succumb to rust, leaf-mould, white-spot, black-spot, and greenfly. There is little point, surely, in chasing up and down the country with a spade and bucket merely in order to give a few dead twigs a nice send-off.

Seeds

Children, I find, are always amazed that everything in the garden was once a little seed; particularly so when the packet of Sweet William they have nurtured so painstakingly is soon burgeoning as an assortment of diseased hollyhocks, mis-shapen sunflowers, chickweed, and an evil-smelling ground-cover that spreads like lava and is almost certainly carnivorous.

In the garden, seeds fall into two categories (a) the cracks in the path, and (b) where starlings have breakfast. To avoid wastage, therefore, grow all seeds in a greenhouse where, if

152

it is properly heated, they will die before they can do any damage.

Water

No garden can possibly flourish without adequate supplies of water. Now is the time of year to cut off the split ends of hoses so that they fit snugly onto the tap, or would if the jubilee clip hadn't rusted solid during the winter with the drip that was coming out of the tap before the pipe burst during the cold snap. Having replaced the upstand pipe, tap, and jubilee clip, bandage the fingers and secure the neatly cut hose; which, as a result of having been neatly cut, will now be some nine inches too short to reach the one bed which requires permanent watering. Never mind, any nurseryman or ironmongers will be able to supply you with an extra length of hose and a connecting-link with which you can easily fail to connect the new bit with the old, since the old is too thick to go into the end of the connecting-link. The best course is to buy an entirely new hose of the required length; there is no other method of finding out that the tap you have just soldered onto the upstand pipe (since you had no means to hand of threading the pipe to take a nut) is itself .05 of a millimetre wider than the hose.

While you're at the nursery/ironmongers, be sure to buy a sprinkler: there are two main varieties, the one that fails to spin round, and the one that fails to sweep from left to right and back again. Personally, I prefer the latter: at least you get half the garden sodden and know which side the shrubs are going to rot. The other variety sets up little oases at random, and it is all too easy, when strolling across a recently watered stretch, to find oneself sinking up to the shin in a tiny local quicksand.

Gardening advice articles

Now is the time of year to stop writing gardening advice articles and move into a tower block.

Counterweight

"I'm quite sure within the next two decades
we shall have all the girls at Woolworth's
with degrees." *Edward Short, MP*

"Nothing much. Went up the Royal Festival same as usual
with Norman."

"That's the skinny biochemist from Smokers Sundries,
innit?"

"Yes. I wore me spotted wincyette with the velveteen bow."

"Nice. Anything good on?"

"Only bloody Arnold Schönberg, that's all!"

"You must be joking, Doreen! Not *Verklärte Nacht* again?"

"Only bloody *Verklärte Nacht* again, that's all!"

"I wouldn't care, it's not even dodecaphonic."

"That's what I said to Norman. It's not even bloody dodecaphonic, I said. It's *early* Schönberg. That's not what I call
value for money, I said."

"You might as well be listening to Stravinsky, Doreen."

"You might as well be listening to bloody Stravinsky. That's
what I said to him. If I'd known, I wouldn't have gone home
and changed. A short skirt's good enough for early bloody
Schönberg."

"What did he say, Doreen?"

"He said it was seminal. He's so bleeding crude sometimes."

"I don't know why you go out with him. He only went to
Trinity College Dublin and his breath smells. It's not as if you
weren't a brain surgeon."

"To tell you the truth, Vera, I—would you mind keeping
your little boy's fingers off them chocolate peanuts, madame,

thank you very much!—to tell you the truth, I'm thinking of giving Norman the bullet. I met this very nice bloke at the Selfridge's Electrical Appliances Department party last Friday—"

"I was going to that, only the cat got into me wigbox Thursday night and did sunnink. How was it?"

"Very nice. It was to commemorate the anniversary of Spinoza's first marriage. They had them little bridge-rolls with roe in them."

"I've always liked Spinoza. You know where you are with the *Tractatus Theologico-Politicus*. He's never flash, is he? If there's one thing I can't stand, it's a flashy determinist."

"I know what you mean. That's exactly what I said to this fella I was telling you about. He works in Plugs & Flex. You wouldn't think so to look at his hands: they're all big, including the fingers. You wouldn't think he'd have the nimbleness for flex."

"I've always liked big hands. You know where you are with big hands. What's his speciality?"

"Ooh, you *are* awful sometimes, Doreen!"

"I din't mean that, you silly cow! I mean, where was he before Plugs & Flex?"

"Balliol. First in Mods, First in Greats. They say he knows more about Kant than anyone on the first floor."

"Doreen!"

"*Immanuel.*"

"There's people looking, Dor. Anyway—"

"Anyway, turns out this fella's got two tickets for the first night of the Bucharest Citizens' Marionette Theatre production of *Aida*, and would I come?"

"You don't half fall on your feet, Doreen."

"I know. It was bloody smashing, Vera! I'd never heard a baritone puppet before. And you know that bit where Rhadames returns in triumph with Amonasro—"

"—the Ethiopian king—"

"—the Ethiopian king, right, well instead of elephants, they had weasels with little rubber trunks on. And all these little puppets were singing in Rumanian!"

155

"Fantastic! What did you do after?"

"Went up Spitalfields, din't we? Had another look at the Christchurch lintels."

"You can't never have enough of Hawksmoor, that's what I always say."

"Well, yes and no. Personally, I never went for the north quadrangle of All Souls."

"I never went for All Souls at all. That bloke who demonstrates artificial lawn's a Fellow of All Souls. He's got a hairpiece. He's a bit funny, if you ask me. There was just the two of us down the stockroom last Wednesday, he come up to me and his face was all shiny, and he was trembling, and I thought: Hallo, Vera, good job you got your body stocking on, and do you know what he wanted?"

"What?"

"He said could he hold my shoes for a bit."

"Go on!"

"Honest."

"What did you say?"

"I said, I'll let you hold one of them, Doctor Strude-Pargiter, but I don't think I ought to go all the way on our first date!"

"Oooh, Vera, you're worse than I am! What did he say?"

"He said he'd written the definitive footnote on the Edict of Worms and he thought that entitled him to certain privileges. So I told him about how my mum would never let me go out with a mediaeval historian, and us ophthalmologists are only happy with our own kind, and I think he understood. I didn't want to hurt his feelings, and I could see the gum running down his forehead with the excitement and everything, so I come upstairs again."

"Very wise. Is it lunchtime yet?"

"Not for another eight minutes and forty-one seconds. Why?"

"I want to go up the travel agent's, don't I? Leave it too late, everywhere's booked up."

"Going anywhere nice?"

"I thought I might try the ten-day cruise of the fjords, only forty-nine guineas, including headphone. You visit sites of the

Old Norse Sagas, and in the afternoons well-known philologists discuss famous textual cruces on deck, if wet in the first-class dining-room. There's semantics every evening, and a gala ball on the Saturday when everyone comes as the troll of his choice and gets rotten drunk. Alice Prior in Plastic Binettes nearly got pregnant twice last year, and she's only ever read *Beowulf* in Penguin, so it just shows you. Tell you what, Vera, whyn't you come with me? It wouldn't half be a giggle, or *gögal*, as the Eddas put it."

"It's ever so nice of you to suggest it, Doreen, but I don't think it's me, really. I think I'll just stay in the library again this year, there's no swimming, of course, but it's warm, and there's always a few people from the British Home Stores boning up on something or other, they're ever such a friendly crowd."

"Vera Collinson, you can't pull no wool over *my* eyes! I know what you're up to, you sneaky bitch, you're working on that thesis of yours, right? *Zygostereopy in The Retina Of The Potto, Clinical Observations Towards A Classification, by Miss Vera Collinson?*"

"Oh, Doreen, I din't want to tell no one, not even you! It's just—you won't take offence?—it's just that I want to, you know, better myself. I want to get on. I don't want to sell Smarties in Woolworth's forever! And if I had a Ph.D., Doreen, I could leave all this behind me, I could make something of myself, I could *be* someone, I could get somewhere!"

"My Gawd, Vera, you're not thinking of . . ."

"Yes, Doreen, Marks & Spencers!"

"You're a mad ambitious little fool, Vera Collinson! But—but I admire you!"

"Don't cry, Doreen, love. There's other things in life, you'll get married, have kids, you see if you don't, it'll all—"

"If only I had the application for original research, if only I had the academic stamina, if only I'd kept up—yes, madame, a quarter of hazelnut cluster, madame, right away, madame, no thank you, madame, quite all right, I just got something in my eye, that's all, madame, that'll be seven pee, thank you very—sob—much."

Father's Lib

"The City University of New York has offered its male staff paternity leave on the same terms as female staff get maternity leave. It is believed to be the first time such a provision has been offered in an American labour contract." *The Times*

There are a number of things that are going to be wrong with this piece.

Some of them will be noticeable—a certain sogginess here and there; a tendency, uncharacteristic in the author, to use one word where two would normally do; arguments, if you can call them that, which start, falter, then peter emptily out; odd bits of disconnected filler, such as laundry lists, a reader's letter or two, notes from the inside cover of my driving licence, a transcript of my tailor's label; that sort of thing.

There will be phrases like "that sort of thing".

Some of the things that are going to be wrong will not be noticeable—the fact that the writer has a tendency to fall off his chair between paragraphs; to knock his coffee into his desk drawer; to rip the trapped ribbon from his typewriter and tear it to shreds, moaning and oathing; to wake up with a start to find the impression 1QA"ZWS/XED @ CRF£V on his forehead where it has fallen into the keys; to light a cigarette while one is still ticking over in the ashtray; to stop dead, wondering where his next syllable is coming from.

Nor will you notice, since the typographer, sturdy lad, will be backing up the young author like a seasoned RSM shoring a pubescent subaltern before Mons, that a good half of the words are misspelled, if there are two "s's" in "misspelled," that is; and if it shouldn't be "mis(s)pelt," anyway.

I'm glad that sentence is over; if it was a sentence. Was there a verb there?

But, for once, ineptitude will be its own defence; inadequacy its own argument. The very fact that readers this week are about to receive (have, indeed, already in part received) a substandard article with the tacks showing and the sawdust trickling out the back only proves the writer's thesis: which is that the concept of paternity leave has been a long time a-coming. That it has come to the United States, pioneer of the ring-pull can, automatic transmission, monosodium glutamate, the Sidewinder missile, and sundry other humanitarian break-throughs should be no surprise to anyone; what is grievous is that there is little sign that the blessed concession is to be adopted on this side of the Atlantic.

Not in time for me, anyhow. And—hang on, that little light on the bottle-warmer that goes out when the teated goody reaches the required temperature has just done so. All I have to do now is unscrew the cap on the bottle, reverse the teat, replace the cap, shake the air out, nip upstairs, prise apart the kipping gums before she's had a chance to wake up and scream the plaster off the wall, whang in the teat, sit back, and,

Dropped it on the bloody floor.

That's what I like about the three a.m. feed—that deftness in the fingers that only comes after two hours deep untroubled sleep, the clarity of the eyes rasping around behind the resinous lash-crust, the milk underfoot due to inability to find slipper and fear of turning on light in bedroom to search for same in case wife wakes up, thereby destroying entire point of self groping around in first place.

I'll come back to the argument in a minute. Now have to boil teat, mix new feed, screw, light goes on, light goes off, unscrew, reteat, rescrew, shake, nip upstairs, prise apart kipping gums, correction, prise apart screaming gums, that's my daughter, five weeks old and more accurate than a Rolex Oyster, it must be 3.01, must get feed done by 3.05, it takes exactly four minutes from first scream for three-year-old son to wake up, where's my panda, where's my fire-engine, I'm thirsty, I'm going to be sick, news that he's going to be sick delivered on high C, thereby waking up wife at 3.09 exactly, wife shouts What's going on? whereupon son shouts Mummy, father shouts Shut up, lights start going on in neighbouring houses . . .

3.04 and fifty seconds, breath coming short and croaky from stairs, got feed mixed, teat boiled, all screwed down, whip out miniature daughter with .001 to spare, pop in teat, falls on it like Peter Cushing on an unguarded throat. I lean back in nursery chair, feet tacky from old milk, left fag burning beside typewriter on kitchen table, know fag will burn down on ashtray rim, like Chinese torture in *Boy's Own Paper*—"When frame leaches thong, Blitish dog, thong tighten on tligger, burret brow blains out, heh, heh, heh!"—fag will fall off ashtray, burn hole in table, possibly burn down house, Family Flee In Nightclothes.

I am actually writing this an hour later, madness recollected in tranquillity, if you can call tranquillity thing involving cat which has woken up in filthy mood to find milk on floor, therefore licking up milk off floor, therefore in middle of floor when I come back to kitchen, therefore trodden on.

Anyhow, back to an hour ago, still feeding daughter, she beginning to drop off halfway through feed, terrible sign meaning can't go on with feed since daughter asleep, can't not go on, because if she goes down half-full, she'll be up again at 4.38, screaming, son up at 4.42, where's my panda, where's my fire-engine, wife up at 4.46, saying If you're incapable of doing a simple thing like a feed etcetera to sleeping form, thereby transforming it into waking form, fall out of bed in netherworld confusion, thinking fag burning house down, look around for something to Flee In, since don't wear Nightclothes, sub-editors all change headlines for 5 a.m. edition, Nude Phantom Terrorises Hampstead Third Night Running.

Wake daughter up, she cries, must be colic, hoist on shoulder, legs all colicky-kicking (I'd like to see James Joyce change a nappy), pat on back, crying goes up umpteen decibels, bring

160

down again, mad gums grab teat, bottle empties like a Behan pint, relief.

Change daughter, all dry, smooth, cooing, give final burp with little rub, daughter hiccups, sick drenches dressing-gown sleeve, daughter's nightdress, change daughter again, can't find new nightdress, walk around numb and sicky, daughter shrieking now, since, having displaced part of feed, requires topping up, else valves will grind or crankshaft seize up, or something, back downstairs with daughter on shoulder wailing, feel like mad bagpiper, mix new feed one-handed, screw, light goes on, light goes off, unscrew, reteat, rescrew, shake, carry out with daughter, slam kitchen door with foot. Wake up cat.

Get upstairs, son wandering about on landing with dismembered bunny, I want a pee, can't explain holding daughter and feeding same is priority, since Spock says AVOID SUCH CLASHES THIS WAY TO JEALOUSY ETCETERA, lead son to lavatory with spare hand, holding bottle against daughter, daughter can now see bottle like vulture over Gobi windows rattle with renewed shrieking, leave son peeing in sleepy inaccuracy on seat, back to nursery, finish feeding daughter, son roars I CAN'T GET MY PYJAMA TROUS-SERS UP, try to rise with daughter, bottle falls, teat gets hairy hammers start in skull, but thanks, dear God, daughter now full, asleep, plonk in crib, turn out light, hurtle sonwards, son not there.

Son in bedroom, shaking wife, I CAN'T GET MY PYJAMA TROUSERS UP.

I creep, broken, downstairs. You know about treading on the cat. I look at the garbling in the typewriter. It stops at "hang on, that little light on the bottle-warmer that goes out." Sit down, smelling of regurgitation and panic, stare at keyboard, listen to dawn chorus going mad, man next door coughing his lung into the receptacle provided, far loos flushing, new day creaking in on its benders.

What I was going to write about before I was so rudely interrupted was, I see from the first tatty gropings, an article about how enlightened America was to introduce paternity leave for new fathers so that they wouldn't have to work for the first few weeks and could help cope with the latest novelty item, instead of going off to the office, the shop, the surgery, the factory.

Or the typewriter.

I had all these great arguments in favour of introducing the system over here, I had all the points worked out, it was all so lucid, so right, so uncounterable: I should bring about an instant revolution.

What arguments they were!

And if I only had the strength left to get them down on paper.

The Workers' Bag Is Deepest Red

> **"The Scottish council of the Labour Party
> today approved almost unanimously a
> policy for the complete nationalisation of
> the vast privately owned Highland estates
> and the salmon fisheries if a Labour
> government is returned to power."**
> *The Times*

I followed the clerk down the eau-de-nil corridor and through
a brown door marked FISH DIVISION: ENQUIRIES.
Inside, a bald man sat at a steel desk beneath a wall-map of the
Highlands pinned with tiny flags and a graph on which a curve
plummeted into its lower margin.

"Man here wants to have a go at the salmon," said the clerk.

The bald man glanced at me over his bifocals.

"Where's your ferret?" he said.

"Ferret?" I said.

"Little bugger with short legs," said the clerk. "Can't half
run, though."

"I know what a ferret is," I said. "But I'm after salmon.
Ferrets go down rabbit holes."

"Funny place to look for salmon," said the clerk. "Still, it
takes all sorts, that's what I always say."

"We can lease you a government ferret," said the bald man.
He reached for a file, wet his thumb, began plucking forms out.
"Need a 121/436/18g, a 72A/ff, and two pound deposit against
loss or damage."

I cleared my throat.

"There seems to be some mistake," I said. "You don't catch
salmon with ferrets."

"He's got a point," said the clerk. "They go down like stones." He indicated the graph. "Salmon production's been dropping off sunnink terrible lately."

"Who told you to use ferrets?" I asked.

The bald man tapped a thick grey-covered book beside his in-tray.

"Come down from Central Division," he said.

"We're radicalising," said the clerk. "And rationalising."

"Sounds to me as though they've got their lines crossed somewhere," I said.

They looked at me.

"Troublemaker here," said the bald man.

"There's channels, you know," said the clerk.

"How you going to catch salmon, then," said the bald man, "without a ferret?"

"Flies," I said.

"Show him out, Sid," said the bald man.

"I don't understand," I said.

"We got work to do," said the bald man, "without comedians."

"I'm serious," I said.

"Pull this one," said the clerk. "It's hard enough training ferrets to jump out of a boat, let alone flies."

"You'd open your jam jar," said the bald man, "and they'd be off. I know flies."

"Look," I said, "you do it with a rod and line. You tie the fly to the hook, you cast the line with the rod, you . . ."

"Ah," said the bald man. He nodded. "Cross purposes here, Sidney. I thought he was talking about salmon. It's grouse he's after."

"You should've said," said the clerk, irritably tearing up his half-filled forms and reaching for a new batch. "And it's not flies, it's worms you use for grouse."

"Don't be ridiculous," I said, "how can you catch a grouse with a worm?"

"Don't ask me," said the clerk, "you're supposed to be the sportsman. We only work here. On attachment."

"From Swindon," said the bald man. "Personally, I prefer trains. You know where you are with trains."

"We're working on a pilot project," said the clerk, "to put grouse on rails. It's up before the Recommendations & Amendments Committee. It could revolutionise the entire industry."

"You'd know when they was coming, then," said the bald man. "None of this hanging about with a worm on the end of a string. You'd just sit there with your timetable, and soon as the 8.40 grouse showed up, bang!"

"With your stick," said the clerk. "Any old stick. Think of the saving!"

"And once you had your rails laid," said the bald man "there's no end to the spin-offs. You could have a dog-track. There's all these hounds we've got, not doing nothing, just walking about and peeing against the van. Train 'em to run after a grouse, you got an entire leisure industry."

"It seems somewhat less than sporting," I said.

The bald man looked at the clerk.

"There's your private enterprise talking, Sidney," he said. "See what I mean? No grasp of basic concepts." He turned back to me. "You don't seem to realise," he said, "what the meat industry entails. Mouths to feed, son, mouths to feed. We got an output target of four million grouse this year. Going over to battery production in August. Biggest aluminium shed complex north of Doncaster."

I sighed.

"Not much sport there, I'm afraid," I said.

"Don't see why not," said the clerk. "You could help with the plucking."

"It's a far cry from shooting," I said.

"I thought we was talking about grouse," said the bald man. "Not trout."

"You *shoot* trout?"

He drew a large buff book from a shelf and threw it on the desk.

"Central Division Beige Paper," he said. "All in there. Results of the Research Division work-study. They went into the question of how you catch these bleeders when they're only in the air about 1.8 seconds, on average. Tried holding nets over the streams, but they're too sharp. Time you've seen 'em and got your wrists going, they're back in the water again. Only way is to lie on the bank with shotguns, soon as they leap, you're on 'em."

"And how, exactly," I said, "do you bring them in?"

"Retrievers," said the clerk.

"Oh, come on." I cried. "Dogs will never go in after fish!"

"Cats will," said the bald man.

"Got him there, Harold!" said the clerk. "He'd never thought of cats."

"Private enterprise again, Sidney. In blinkers. Hidebound by tradition. Good enough for daddy, it's good enough for me, what? This is 1971, mate!"

"4," said the clerk.

"1974," said the bald man.

"And how do you propose," I said, "to train cats to swim?"

"Listen," said the bald man. "If you can train flies, we can train bloody cats."

"I think I'll be going," I said, and stood up. They stared at my waders. "For trout," I explained.

"First good idea you've had," said the clerk. "The nettles are terrible."

"Hallo," said the bald man, glancing suddenly past us, and pushing his spectacles up his nose, "the stock's arrived." He rose.

I followed them to the window. Between the administration building, on the fourth floor of which we stood, and the Amalgamated Ghillie Union tower block opposite, ran a bright tarn that had risen in some now invisible mountain. Beside it, a dump truck was unloading a wriggling pile of small silver fish directly into the hurtling water. Upon entering which, they all turned belly-up. I peered, but we were fifty feet above.

"There's something wrong with those trout," I said.

"Shows how much *you* know," said the clerk. "They're pilchards."

166

"Calls himself a sportsman," said the bald man.

"But pilchards are saltwater fish!" I cried.

"And very popular, too," said the clerk. "On toast, with a bit of tomato sauce."

"But they're all dying!"

"So I should hope," said the bald man. "Easy to see he's never tried packing six pilchards in a tin, innit, Sidney?"

"If you did it his way," said the clerk, "it'd take six weeks to get the lid on. They hop about like nobody's business, pilchards."

"Prob'ly never seen a tin," said the bald man, jabbing a thumb at me. "His lot prob'ly hunt pilchards on horseback."

The clerk thought about this for a moment or two.

"Doubt it," he said at last, "you'd have a hell of a job aiming."

The bald man nodded, slowly.

"Common sense, really," he said.

Good God, That's Never The Time, Is It?

The weather would pick tonight to break. Just when I thought the whole dread moment might pass unnoticed, one day sliding into another without even a perceptible click. And now the sky is full of thunder, lightning, raindrops the size of golf balls, and hot golf balls, at that, dogs are going mad in the explosions, the cat's under the stairs, nightbirds are shrieking themselves hoarse at the thought of all those worms belting up through the topspit to greet the end of the drought . . . the entire galaxy is rotten with augury. If this were Fiji instead of Hampstead, you wouldn't be able to see for flying beads, there'd be blokes jumping up and down on hot coals, and senior civil servants tuning in to their local volcanoes to see what had set the gods off this time, and remittance men from the Home Counties sweating the stitches out of their seersucker suits and praying that the demented house-boy's kris might find an alternative place in which to sink itself.

It can't all be because I shall be thirty-five at midnight. I don't know Anyone with that kind of pull.

I had intended the whole thing, as I say, to pass unnoticed. Thought I'd go to bed at around eleven, aged thirty-four, and wake up in the morning with it all over. Like having your appendix out. Never expected to sit through midnight, June 26, watching everything turn into mice and pumpkins. And here I am, an hour off the end of Act One, and can't sleep for the thunder rattling the rooftiles, threatening the gutters.

I'll be fifty-eight when the mortgage is paid off. Pass like a flash, those twenty-four, all right, twenty-three years, if I'm any judge. Last twenty-three went by like *that*.

Sorry for the paragraph break. I snapped my fingers at *that*, and pain shot all the way up to the elbow; no doubt, arthritis sets in at thirty-five. A few years ago, I could snap my fingers, oh, a dozen times on the trot. Where was I (senility setting in, too, half a million brain cells been conking out annually since twenty-one, that's seven million brain cells, wonder how many I started with, maybe the entire skull is empty, like those joke ashtrays where you put the fags in the eye-sockets, just a couple of doz assorted brain cells left, huddling together like stranded amoeba, watching one another die)? Oh, yes, about the shooting-by of twenty-three years—I was twelve. I can still feel being twelve. Looking forward to the Festival of Britain. I went down to watch the Skylon going up, in short trousers. Me, that is; the Skylon went around in a sort of tin slip. I can exactly recall the feeling of chapped legs, wind coming over Waterloo Bridge. I went up the Shot Tower and spat off it. Tonight, I feel as if the spit hasn't hit the ground yet—*twenty-three years?*

Of course, thirty-five may not be significant at all. I might go on to ninety-six, in which case I ought to be writing this article at forty-eight, i.e. in about ten minutes time. The thing is, one thinks in terms of three score years and ten. It's about all I have left of formal religious belief. That and a lingering guilt about non-payment of fares. One of the few things I don't have instant recall over: what it was like to believe in God. Stopped believing circa 1953, don't know why.

Other things I find it impossible to remember, (1) Virginity (2) What it was like not smoking (3) Being unable to drive (4) Not shaving.

The point is, am I about to become half-dead, or should I consider myself as being half-alive? I am extremely aware of deterioration tonight; I can see it spilling over the belt, feel it when I run my fingers through my hair. It's a short run, these days, barely get off the blocks and you're through the tape. Also, I appear to have more moles on my forearms than heretofore. I may be growing gnarled: finger-joints seem to be taking on angles, quite arbitrarily, which probably explains why my typing has been falling off. It's as accurate as ever, but the fingertips whang down on the neighbouring keys as often as not. Line up on a "g" and an "f" appears on the paper.

Eleven-thirty.

Deterioration is the last thing I worry about, normally. What I feel most is psychic age. It manifests itself most clearly in the sudden awareness that one is actually part of history, and therefore disappearing fast. I look at old newsreels, Stalin and Roosevelt and Churchill chuckling away at Yalta, it could be an eon ago, it might as well be the Treaty of Utrecht they're wrapping up, they could be ceding Mercia to Wessex, it's all dead time; but I was *alive when they did it*, six, going on seven, fully formed, you can see it in the school photographs, same head. I'd already seen Hatfield House, had teeth filled, eaten Radio Malt, fallen in love, caught fish. At bloody Yalta!

We all got a plate from George VI and a framed message congratulating us on our war effort. George the Sixth—it looks like William Rufus, when you write it down. Twenty years since the Coronation, we bought our first telly for it, 12" Murphy with doors, somewhat larger than a wardrobe, used to stand oakenly in the corner like a coffin at an Irish wake, blowing valves faster than you could say Joan Gilbert; twenty years, and I can recall the exact clatter of Muffin's hooves on the piano-lid as if it was . . . in twenty years' time, I'll be fifty-five, Without A Pension I Really Do Not Know What I Shall Do.

It isn't that thirty-five is old in itself; merely that it is, as it were, the hinge, Halfway House, with Death sitting in the snug, biding his time over a brown ale, under the clock. An index of what's left, how long it will take, life's little Rorschach, you just fold it across the middle, and each mirrored blot is thirty-five years long. Or short. I got here so quickly; I was at Oxford yesterday, took O-levels Monday morning, learned to ride a two-wheeler over the weekend, and was it Friday I was dry all night, for the first time? I can't be sure, but I remember my father was in uniform; an old man, nearly thirty.

I wish more had changed, it would endow my degeneration with more significance; jet travel, sliced bread, colour TV, automatic transmission, professional tennis, and golf on the Moon—it isn't much, really. I would like, I don't know, England's coastline to have altered beyond all recognition, dolphins to have taken over the world, something of that order. I'd like to have had an Ice Age or two, been through the Jurassic Period, watched man climb down from the tree, grow less prognathous, discover the wheel—"*Hey, Al, you'll never believe this, ha-ha-ha, I just made something that rolls downhill!*" I don't seem to have been here very long, that's all, and shan't be for much longer.

It could be my fault, of course; maybe I ought to have done more. Not that I haven't done a considerable amount, I've eaten almost everything there is to be eaten, play most card games passing well, visited all forty-nine of the continental United States, written four million words, many of them different. But nothing solid. Mozart, Keats, Jesus Christ, Bix Beiderbecke, they were all dead by this point. "And now, ladies and gentlemen, here to introduce his new opera, *The Eve Of St. Agnes*, is Alan Coren, son of God and first cornet."

Can't be sure it'd be any better, of course. Achievement need not be a hedge against decay. Look at Ozymandias; or, to be more precise, his feet. I grow melancholic (it is five to midnight) at a thought no more complex than that I like it here; it's a good dance, a good movie, a good match, and I glance at my watch and discover that it's half-way gone already: life's little irony number eight, there's no pleasure, however intense, that cannot be flawed by a brief reflection upon its inevitable transience.

Midnight. There we are, then. I'll be all right in a minute. Feel better already, as a matter of fact. Well, it's easier downhill, if nothing else.

Will Ye No Come Back Again?

Feel like Yeats ("I hear lake water lapping with low sounds by the shore/While I stand on the roadway or on the pavements gray . . ."), standing on pavements gray outside Heathrow, just back from two weeks sailing through Greek islands, still feel deck moving under feet, water sloshing against porthole, wind smacking cheeks; can't get land legs, swaying about looking for taxis, horizon moving through thirty degree arc, people staring at strange bandy figure, seems to have limps in both legs, keeps bracing itself against road, grabbing lamp posts, been knocking back cheap inflight gin no doubt, what matter with his face, looks like parboiled hamburger, some brown, some pink, skin flakes following in small cloud; always happens on return from sun, expensive tan starts cracking at customs, like old wallet, begins peeling at luggage bay, by time cab-rank reached, whole face fallen off.

Exhilaration still there, though, despite fist-sized hole in suitcase (gollywog's head poking out, present for small daughter, will Immigration think midget Pakis being smuggled in?), feel fit, slimmer, relaxed after fifteen days unthink, much sleep, no work, stress, editors, children, traffic, slates falling off roof, phones, bills, pets, ready for hurling self into work, writing off debts, New Life . . . rick neck getting cases into taxi, fingers trapped between case and seat, what matter with face? says cab-driver (thinking: what disease this lurching fool brought back from alien parts? Will own skin start falling off tomorrow, will all contacts start reeling about and grabbing for support, is this what cholera like, swamp fever, beri-beri?)

Chugging along M4, sultry night (England in middle of heat-wave, cab-driver twice as brown as either of us, been eighty degrees in Ilford, ha-ha-ha, never cost me a bob), wife excited at prospect of fetching farmed-out infants, got precise timetable, pick them up just before bedtime, whip home, mutual joy, presents (got son Greek machine-gun; son now got machine-guns from eight different countries, nursery look like IRA bunker, what will prison psychiatrists say when son thirty and doing ten years for GBH?), that the trouble with precise time-tables, never take into account Rover 2000 lying sideways across two lanes, fire-engines, police, cars piled up on hard shoulder, hour delay; never mind, ho-ho-ho, these things sent to try us, damn good holiday, see kids tomorrow, put feet up at home tonight, why not open sealed Athens Duty-Free Shop bag, take comforting slug of scotch? Open bag, one bottle cointreau, one bottle something called vεxταp, not our bag, who got whisky, never drink cointreau, as for vεxταp, what is it, could be Greek after-shave, lighter-fuel, anything. Ah well, never mind, make good presents, must know someone who drinks vεxταp, or puts it on dahlias, or something. Nearly had small row, though, who was minding bloody bag, who was looking for bloody taxi, etcetera, what the hell, damn good holiday, great to be home, looking forward to hot bath, clean sheets, yum yum and similar rubbish.

Arrive home; still standing (always expect charred ruin, like *Gone With The Wind*, where Number 26? we ask, old black retainer wiping eyes, Dey done took it fo' a Confed'ate fort, massah, hittin' it wid de cannon all de liverlong night...). Ring doorbell (never take keys on holiday, bound to lose in some flyblown hotel, next thing you know house crawling with Greek burglars), no reply. Funny, should be housekeeper there, big smiles, kettle boiling, where housekeeper, not Bingo night, must be watching box, ring doorbell again, no reply, look at wife, wife look back, wife puts down bags, goes next door, rings bell, neighbours emerge, much bonhomie (such as: What matter with face?), where housekeeper, we say, housekeeper gone, they say, Bingo, we ask, last week, they reply. Rush into neighbour's house, phone mother-in-law, much hemming and hawing, eventually transpires mother-in-law Having Words with housekeeper, housekeeper gave self ten minutes notice, goné forever.

Rush out of neighbour's house (tearing shirt on rose bush, since garden path moving through thirty-degree arc), tell wife, wife shriek, drop bag with bottle of νεκ⊤αp, strange smell infiltrate night; how to get in house, keys with housekeeper, rush round back to break window, no need, back door open, last act of revenge, no doubt hoping Greek burglars arriving anyway, on offchance; peer into house, if not Greek burglars, could be muggers, vandals, Provos taping bombs to lavatory seats, maybe squatters (see long court case stretching out, hippies retaining John Mortimer, self got elderly family solicitor, no match for swinging QC, entire family walking streets behind self holding tin cup), but no sound inside. Go in, terrible noise, thing leap at me, it is Percy, world's most affectionate neutered ginger tom, now a mad thing like small cougar, all claws and malevolence; left to forage for self by vindictive housekeeper, Percy now trust no-one, been living off land like Viet Cong cat, also probably brooding on where to lay blame for neutering, I step back, Percy spring past, vanish into night, looking for sheep to savage, or something.

Open front door, let wife in, wife heavy with gloom, housekeepers like gold dust these days, wife due back at work tomorrow, what going to happen to house, kids, etcetera? Unanswerable questions, drag cases upstairs, house thick with old leaves blown through left-open windows, spiders, wasps; open bedroom door, no sheets on bed. Drop cases, sit on bed, stare at floor, get up, run bath, remove clothes, walk into bathroom, put foot in bath, withdraw foot, stare at foot, foot icecold. Put fingers under tap, tap say H, water say C, turn off tap, pass wife in kitchen staring at coagulated blob, remains of pigeon brought in by cat during some atavistic frenzy (or else, urbanely, as calculated insult), pass on to boiler room, boiler cold, phone Gas Board, come off it, says Gas Board, it ten o'clock on a Sunday night, what about Thursday week, no promises of course?

Start boiling saucepans (all full of old food, brazed on by ex-housekeeper with spot-welder), one bath equals forty saucepans, arms feel like yesterday's spaghetti by time bath full, get into bath, bath now cold again, bits of very old steak and so forth floating about, get out of bath, pull plug, dry cold self on dressing-gown (where towels?), bath-water not going away, plughole full of meat, get meat out with fingers, drop in loo, flush, meat swirl, swim back gamely to surface, shut lid, leave bathroom, wife sitting on bed holding headless golly, head no doubt ripped off when decabbing case, gutter outside house now got small black head in, no doubt, like voodoo sign. Very appropriate, all things considered.

Go to bed.

Wake up, shave cold, rest of face come off in razor, flush loo, watch meat hurtle about again, shut lid, go to start car to fetch kids, car go yergh-yergh-yergh, battery flat, call cab, wife departs childwards, no room for self plus wife plus children plus cot plus pushchair plus cases plus all other junk due back with offspring. Go out into garden, garden look like Matto Grosso, must be crashed Dakota in it somewhere, expect Ronald Reagan to come hacking across lawn any minute behind machete; come to small clearing, find cat dragging wing across it, cat look at me and look at wing as if working out which meatier, cat growl finally and slope off into undergrowth. Get to fishpond, three fish floating in it, belly-up and covered in white spores; suddenly, oh my God, remember Doris Maurice! Doris Maurice is tortoise, so-christened by four-year-old son since no-one knew whether it Doris or Maurice, tortoise-sexing not being family talent, go to tortoise-run behind greenhouse, discover matter of sex purely academic now, as Doris Maurice look extremely deceased. Rotten housekeeper, tortoise needs water daily, pick up Doris Maurice, little legs stay outside shell, no panicky withdrawal, look at little face, Doris Maurice dead as doornail. What to tell small son, maybe small son forget Doris Maurice during stay at Grandma's?

Fat chance. Still standing there when small son return, fighting way through jungle, only thing small son forget is father, Where's Doris Maurice? Have had foresight to prop

Doris Maurice against fence, like shot legionnaire in *Beau Geste*, dead tortoise almost indistinguishable from live tortoise, after all, small son rapidly lose interest, we return to house, cat lunges at us, but we get through back door, son grab Greek machine-gun and run upstairs firing, I inform wife of demise, wife very practical girl, instantly goes into pros and cons of burial, suppose mad cat dig it up, drag it in house, that sort of thing.

Decide to put Doris Maurice in polythene bag in dustbin, wife break down, everyone in house very attached to DM, guaranteed (virtually) by Palmer's Pet Stores to last two hundred years (man in shop said one in Regent's Park remembers Captain Cook, bet Captain Cook wouldn't put tortoise in dustbin, says wife, that man had vision . . .). No polythene bag, all we have is Athens Duty-Free Shop bag, put Doris Maurice in, put in dustbin.

Worry. Suppose knock on door next week, policeman there with pitiful cargo, Excuse me, sir, is this your . . . Probably by-laws against such disposal, health risk, RSPCA complaints. Either that or some dustman totting for goodies in for terrible shock, opening Athens Duty-Free Shop bag hoping for cheap fags, gin, maybe even vεxτap, and what he find? Doris Maurice. Shock could kill; unless he take Doris Maurice for weird souvenir, Greek delicacy, or not even real tortoise, but stone one (not much difference), take home, put on mantelpiece.

Stand at window, looking at dustbin. Feel as though last went on holiday about eight years ago. Always the way, though. Bet if Yeats went back to Innisfree, he'd find all his beans withered, and the clay and wattles fallen off the roof, and the bees all dead, dried up like trout flies, and the linnet's wings being dragged through the gloaming by the cat.